Cartoon animals

Coloring Book

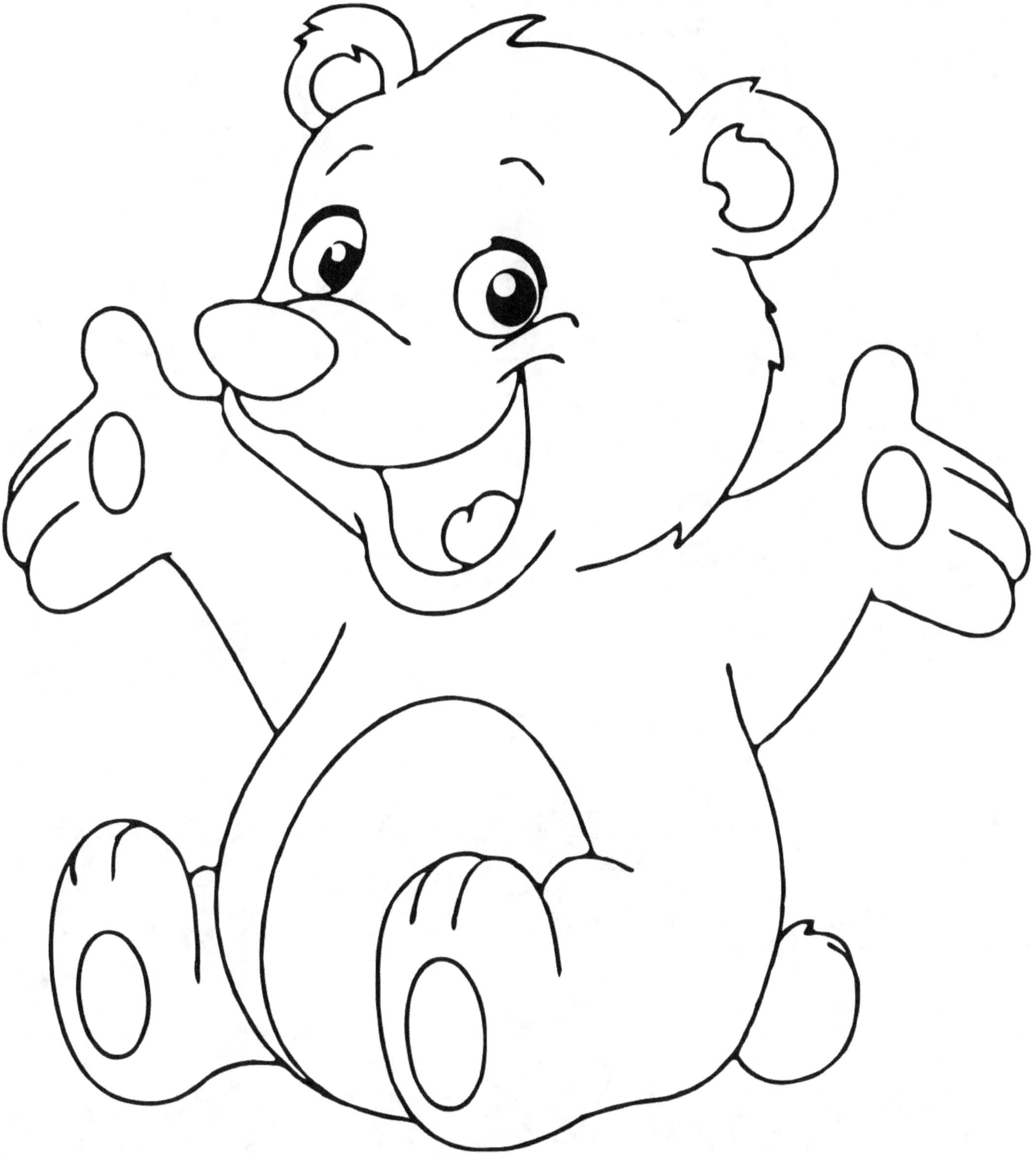

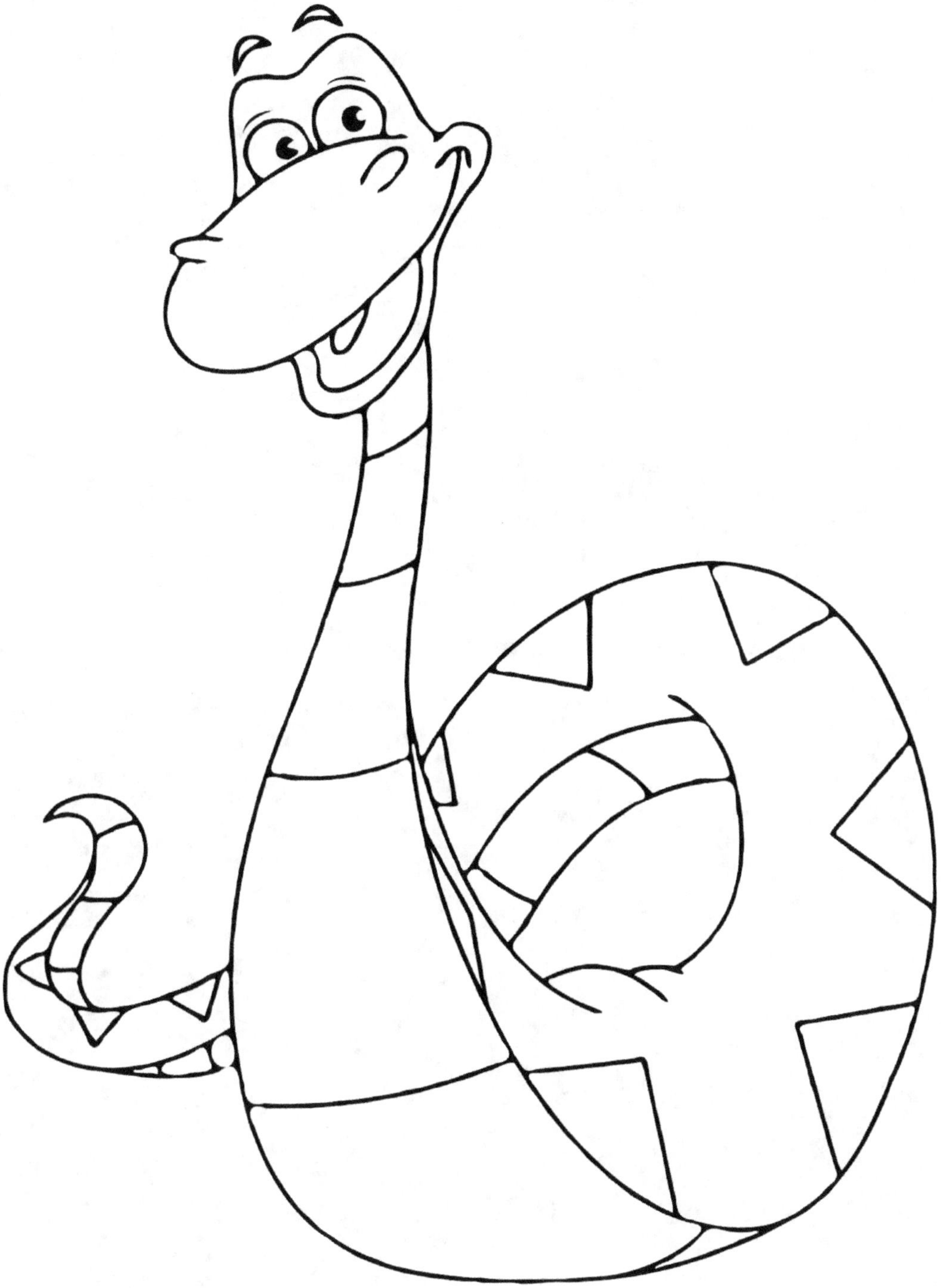

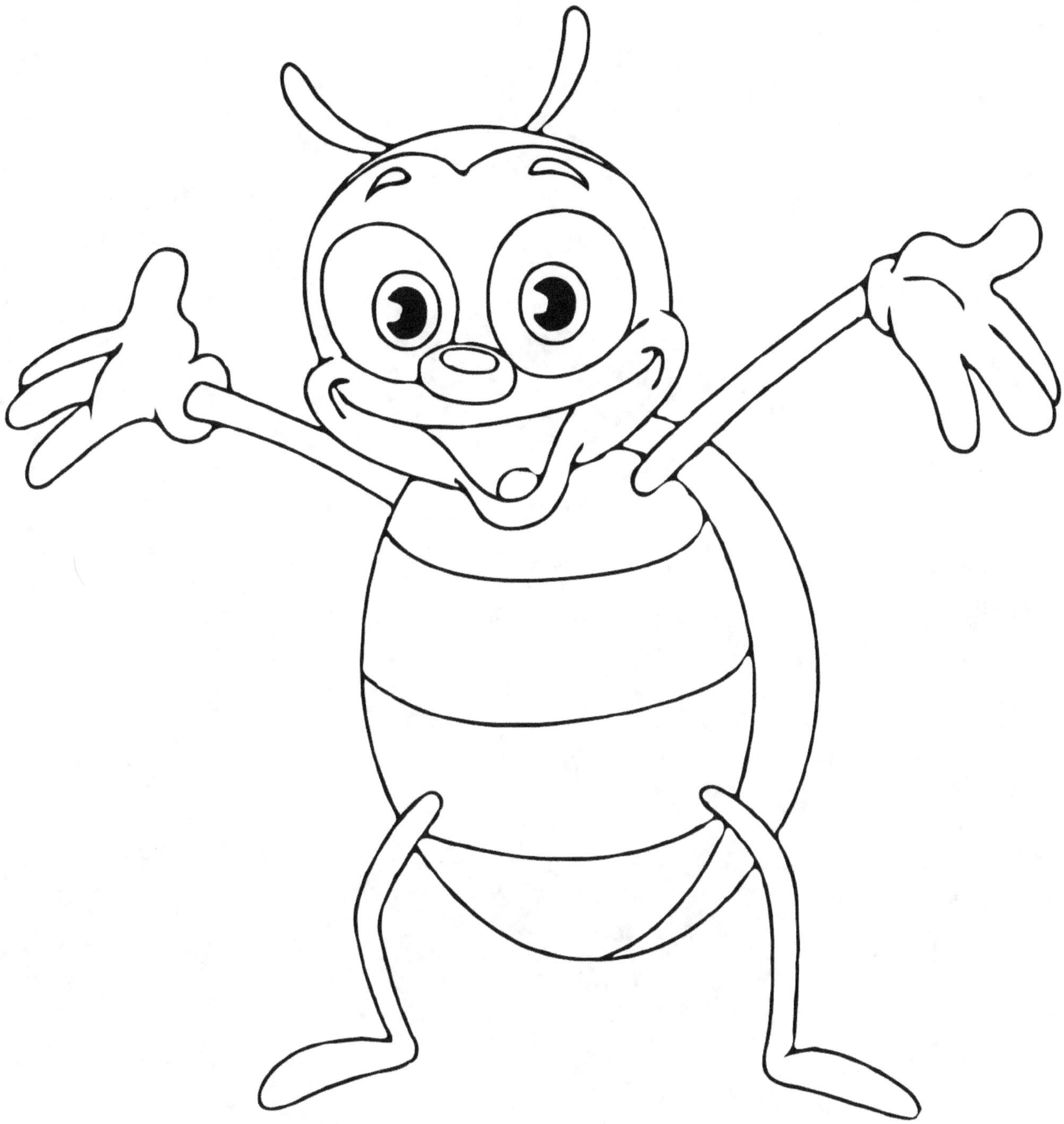

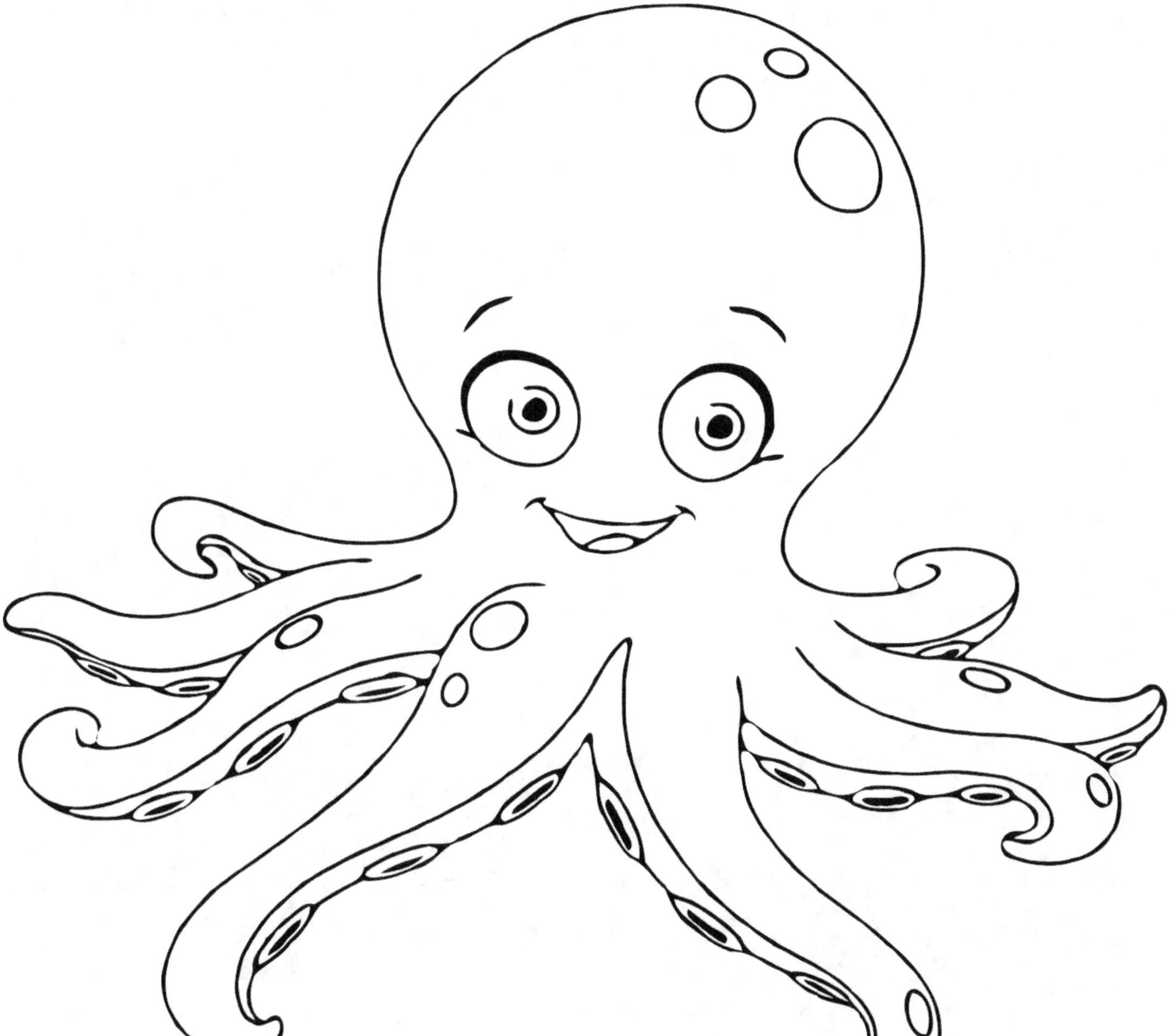

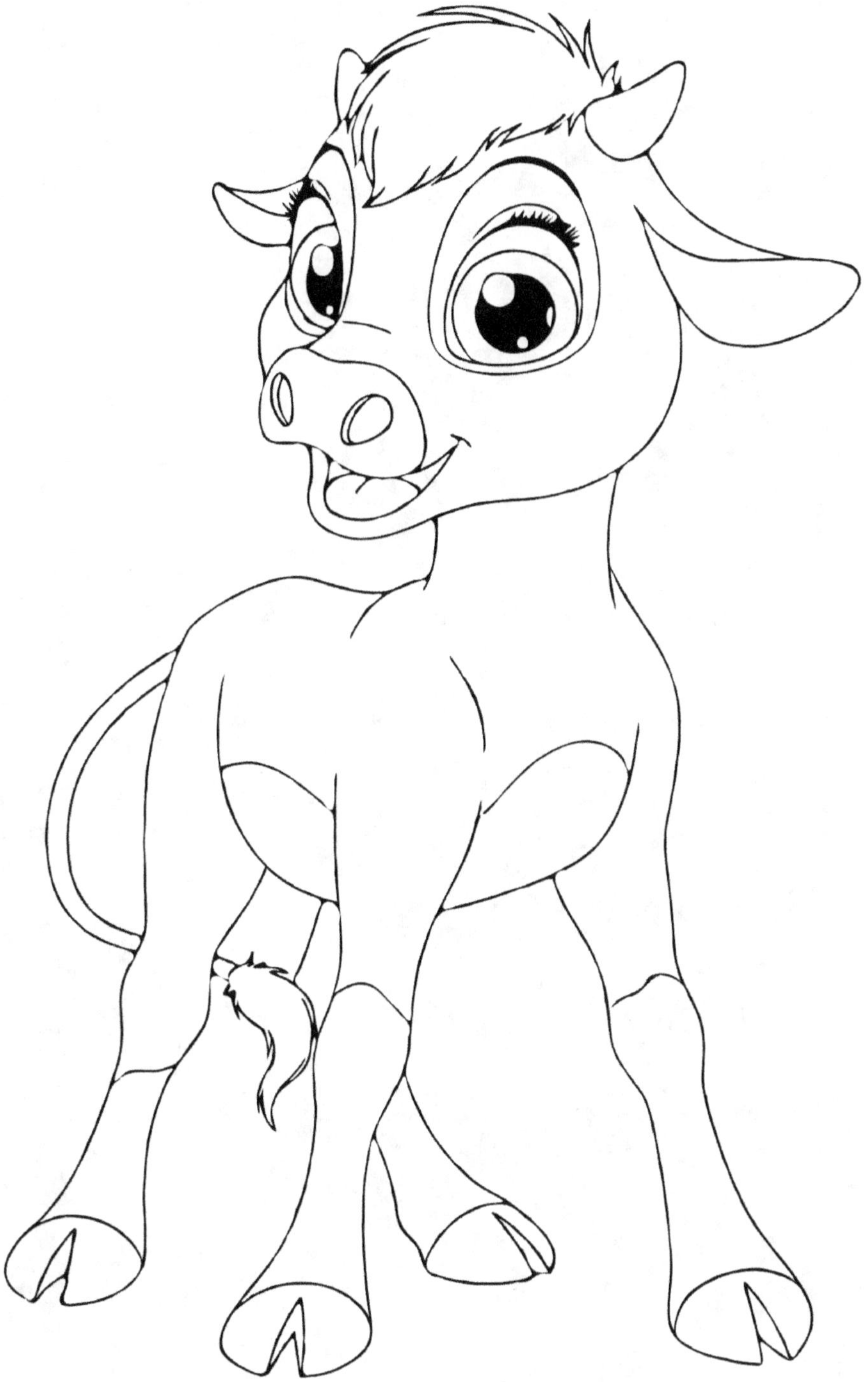

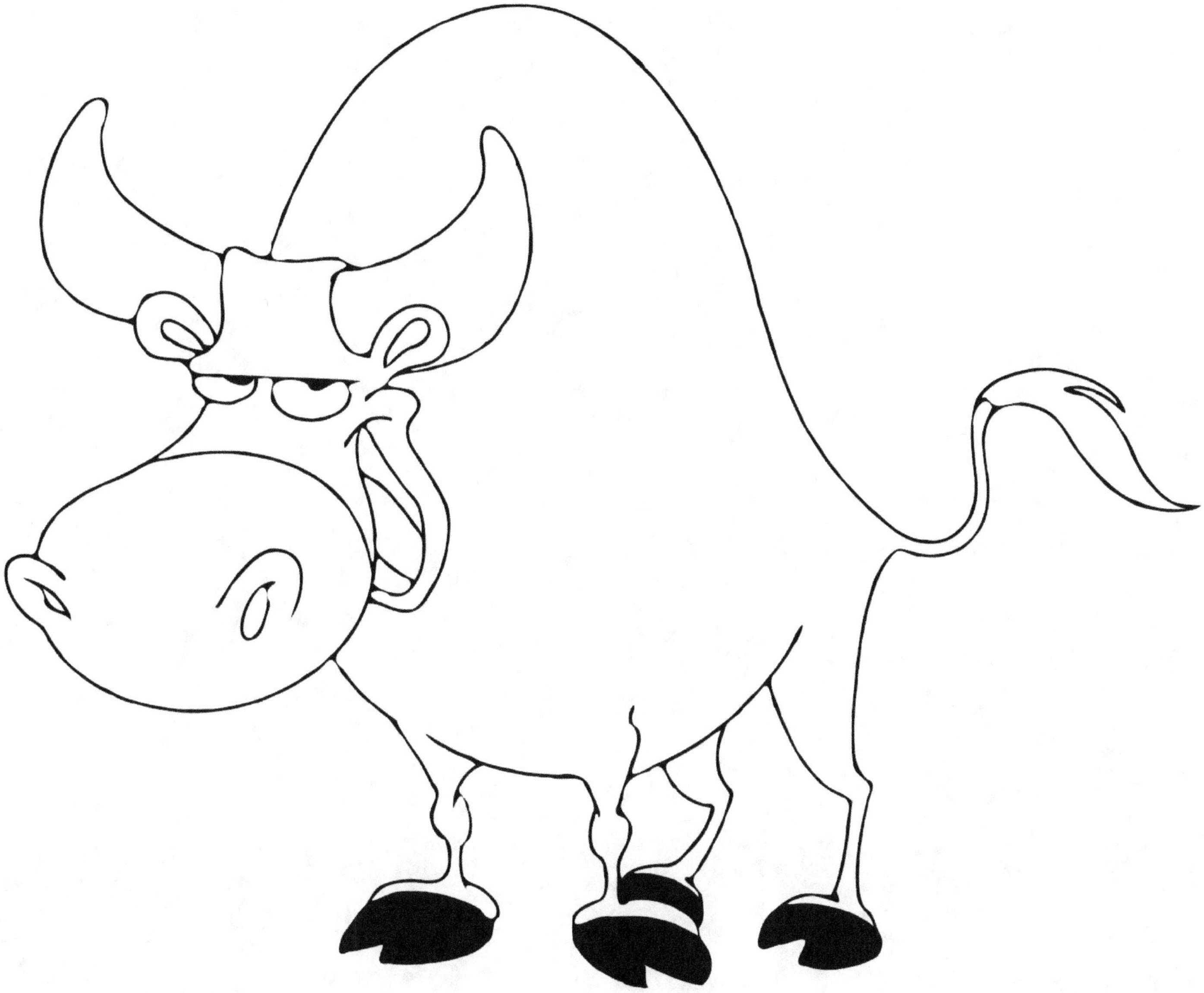

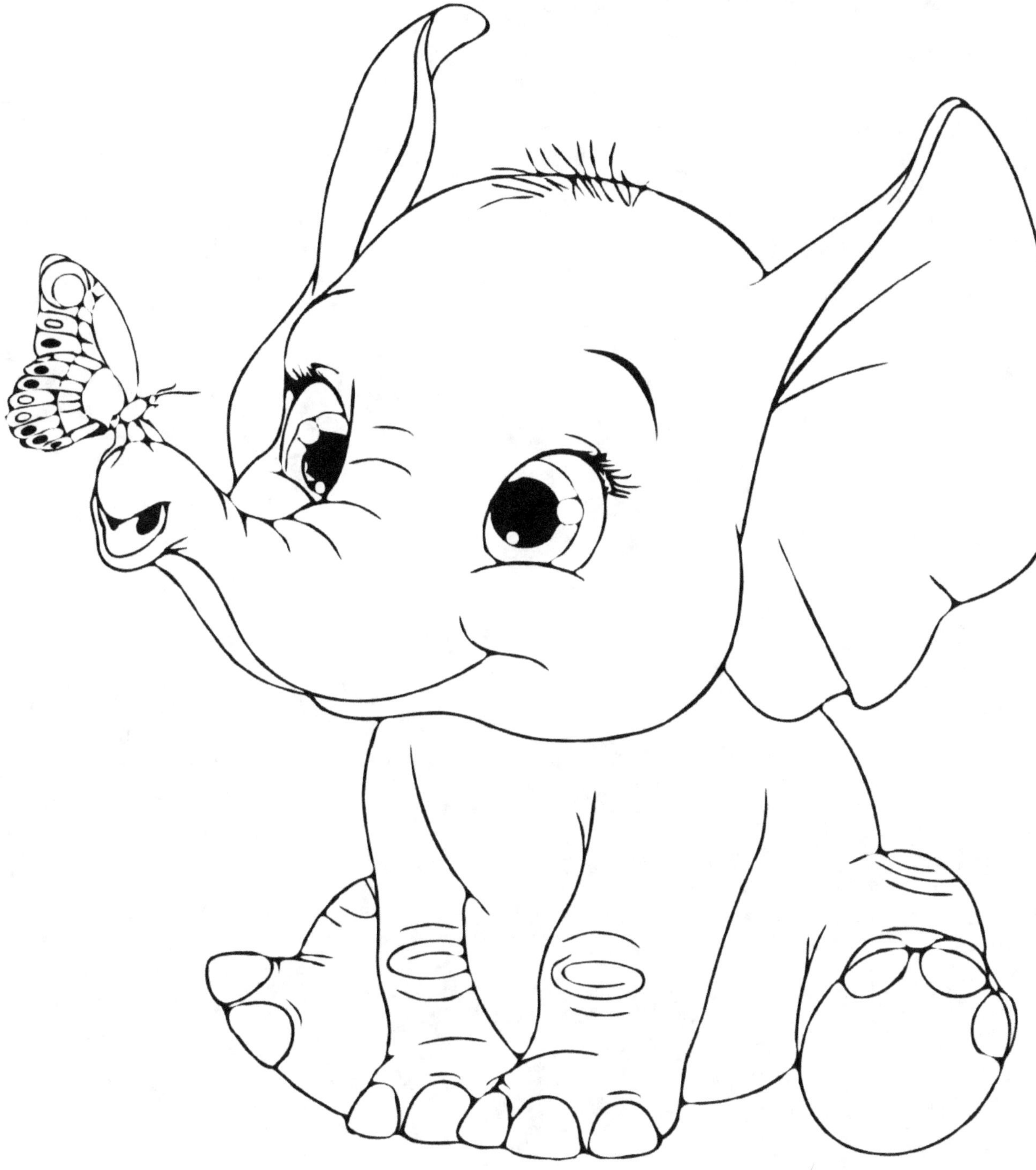

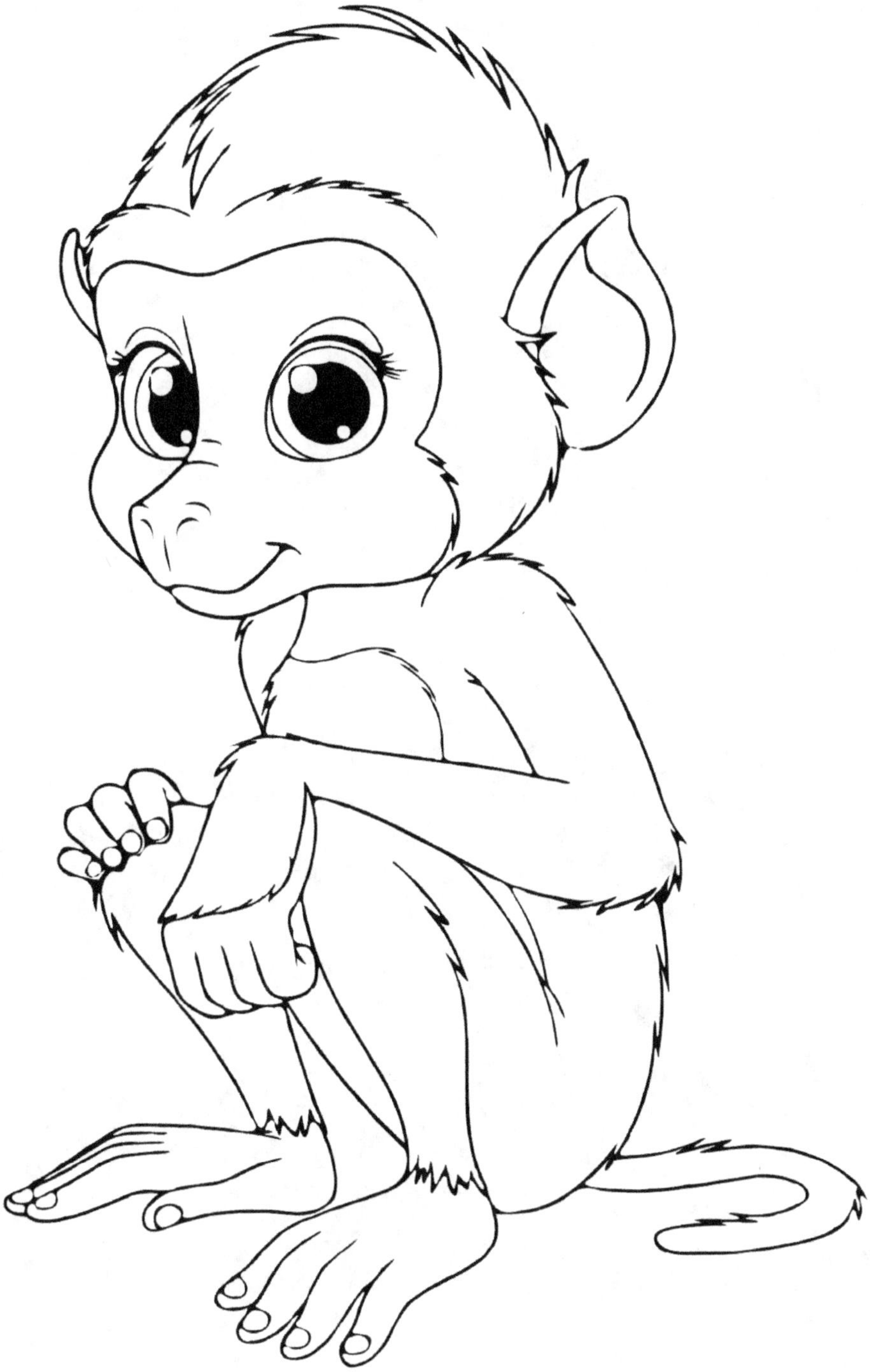

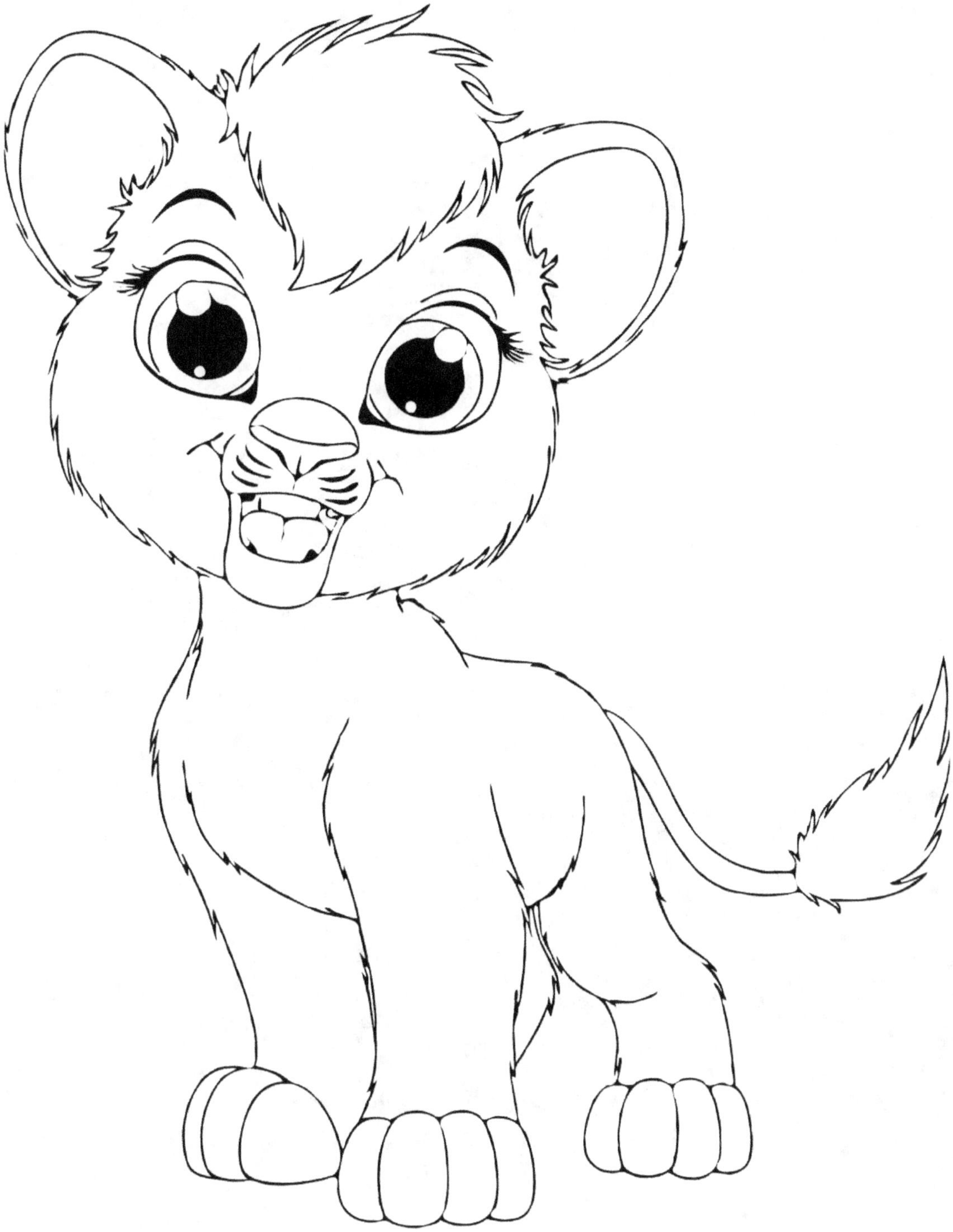

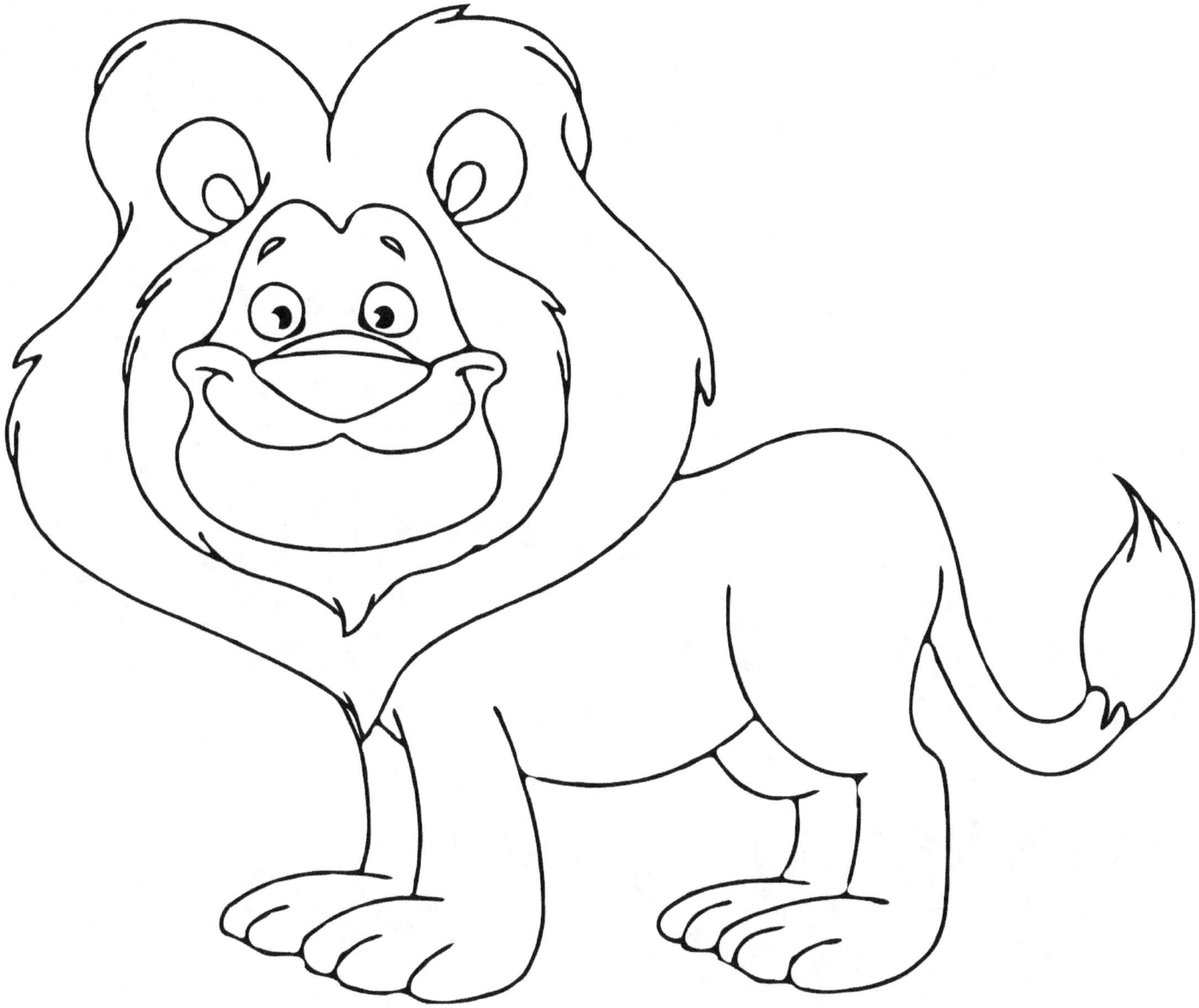

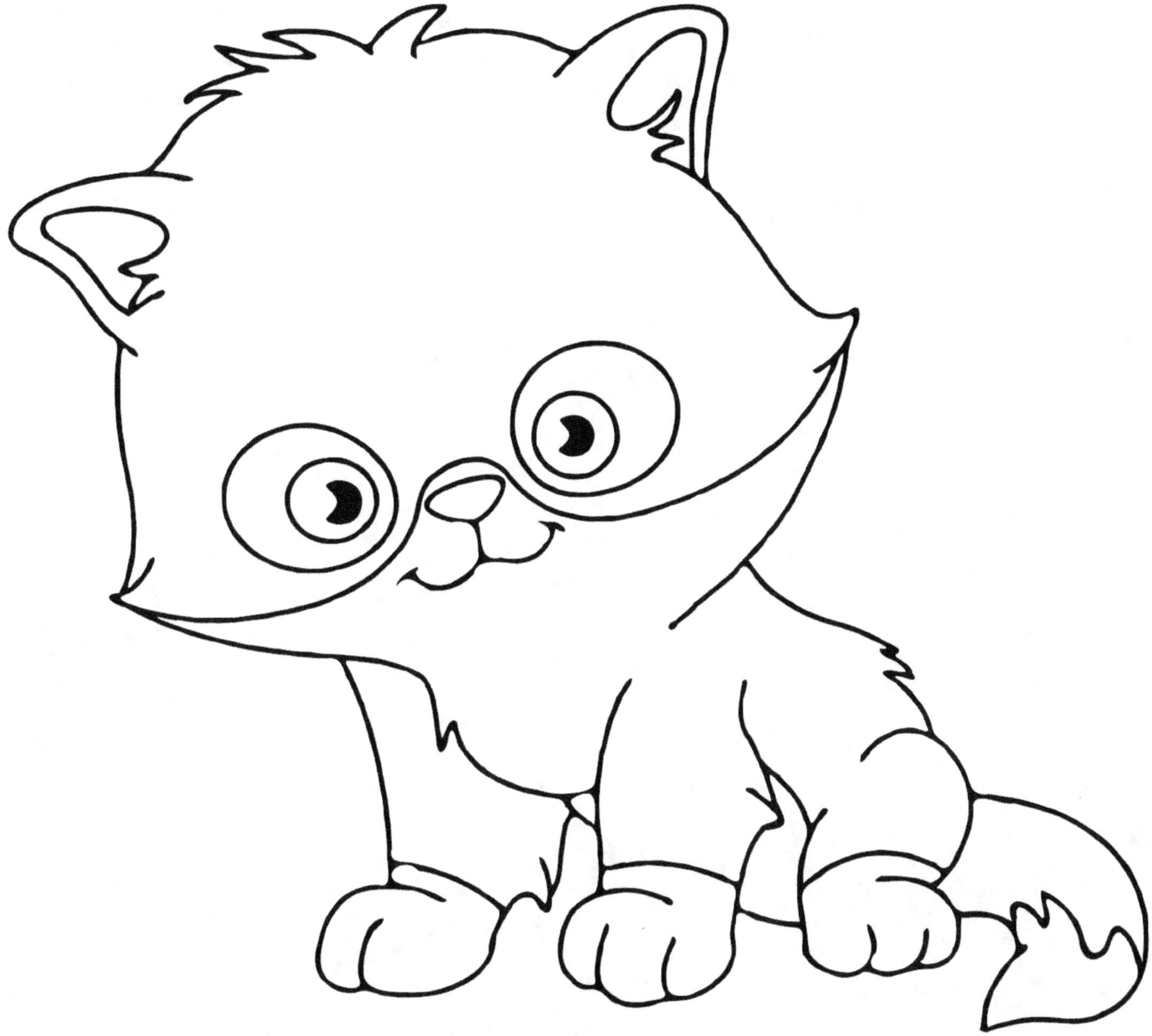

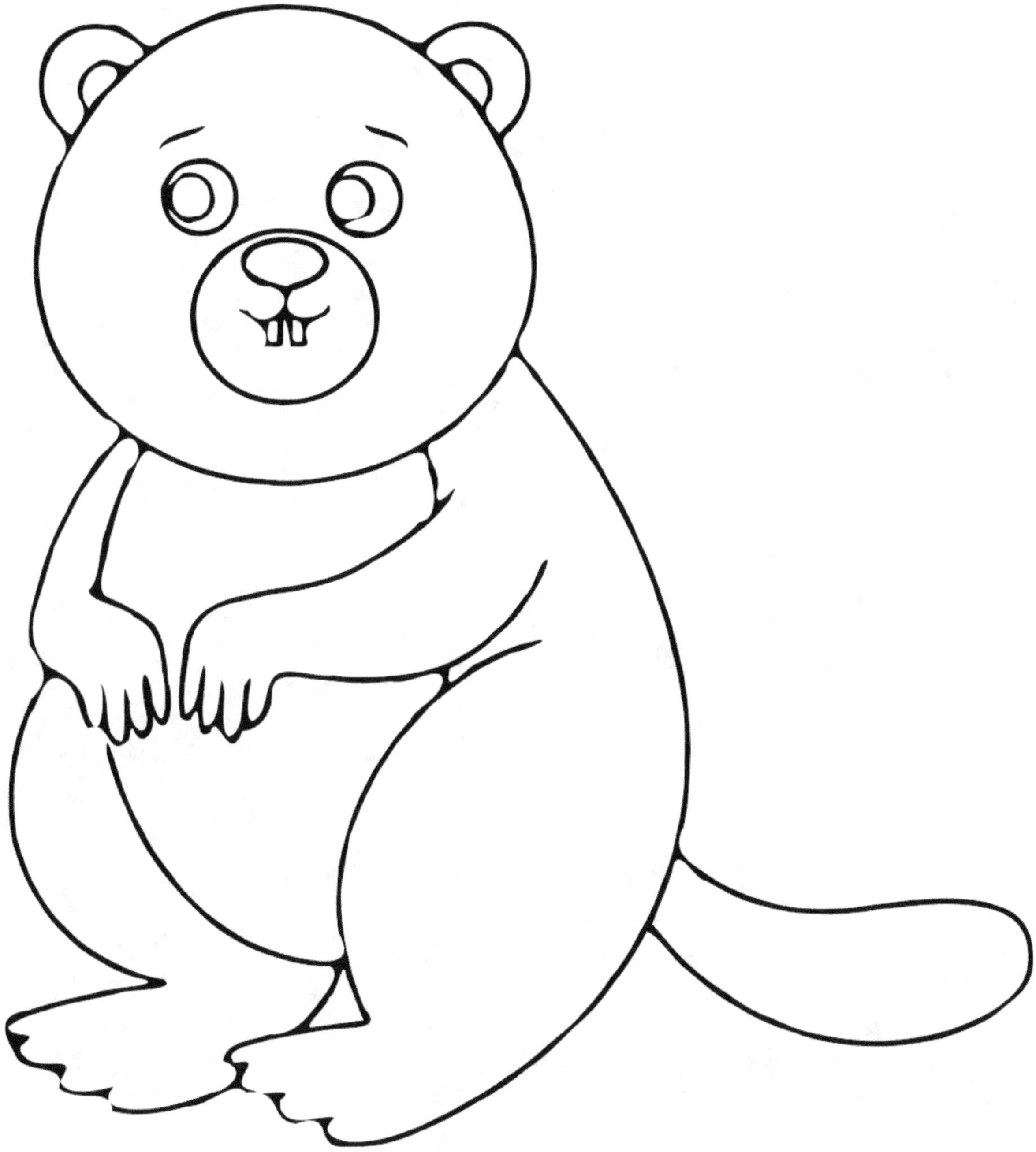

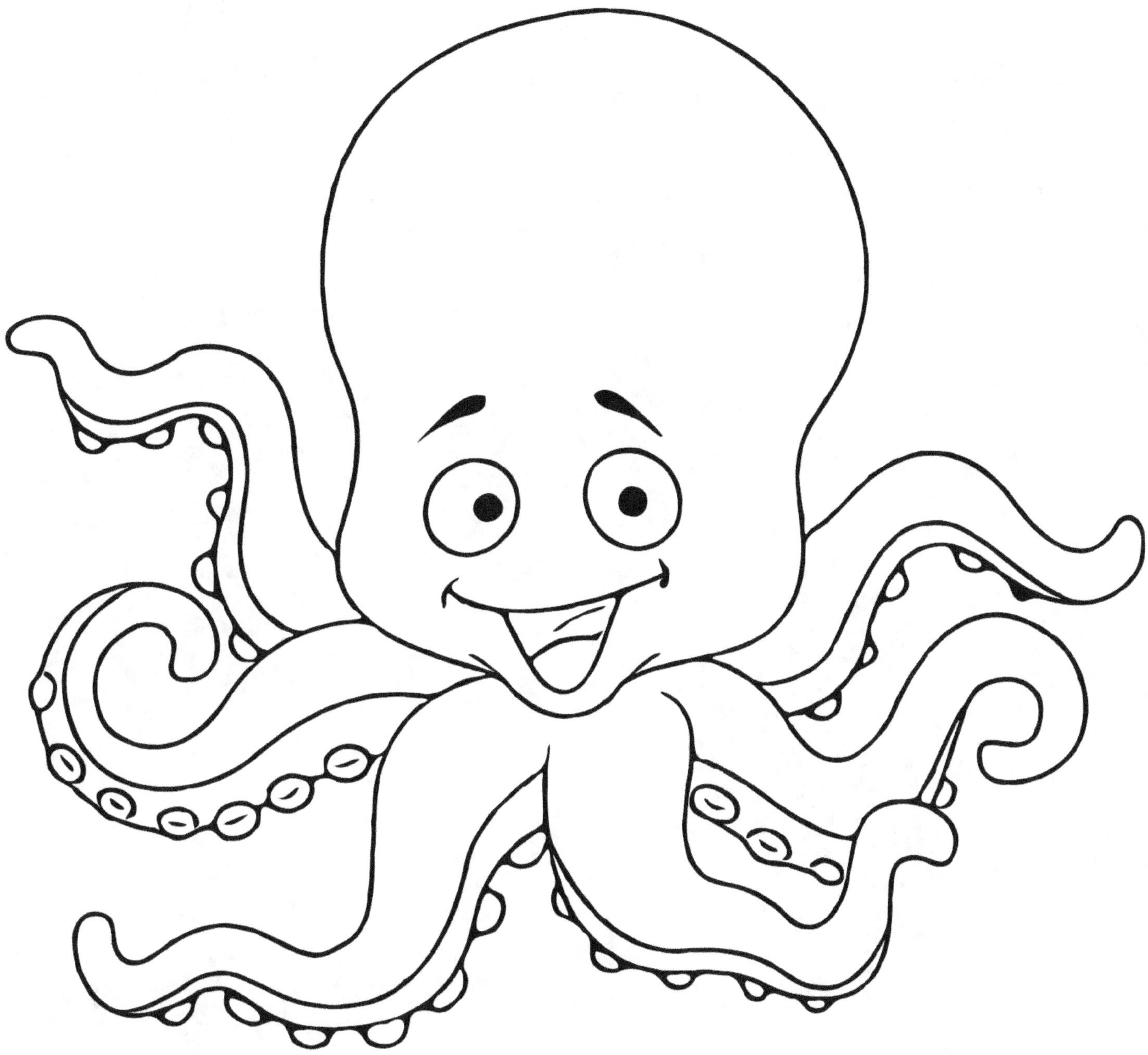

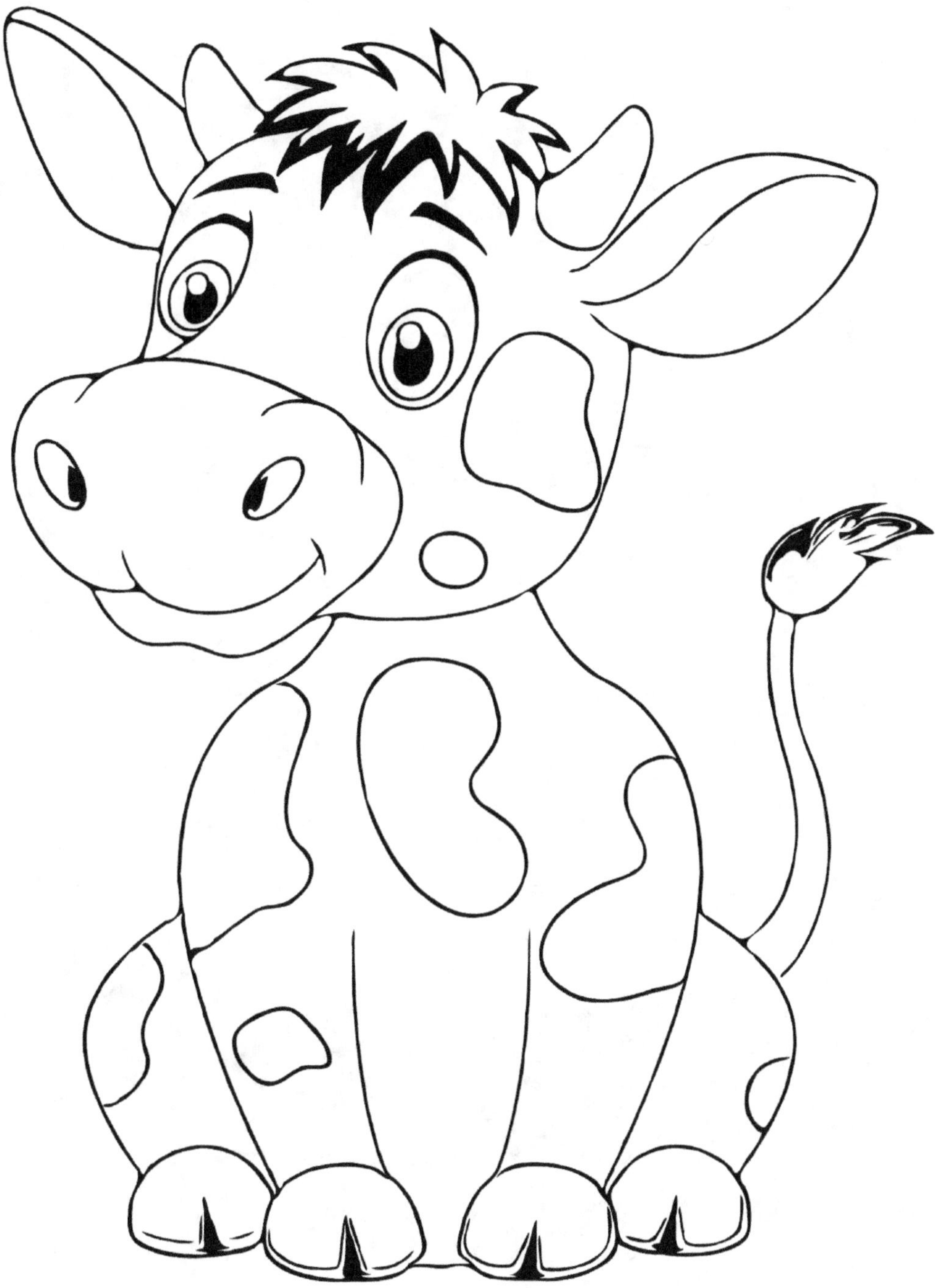

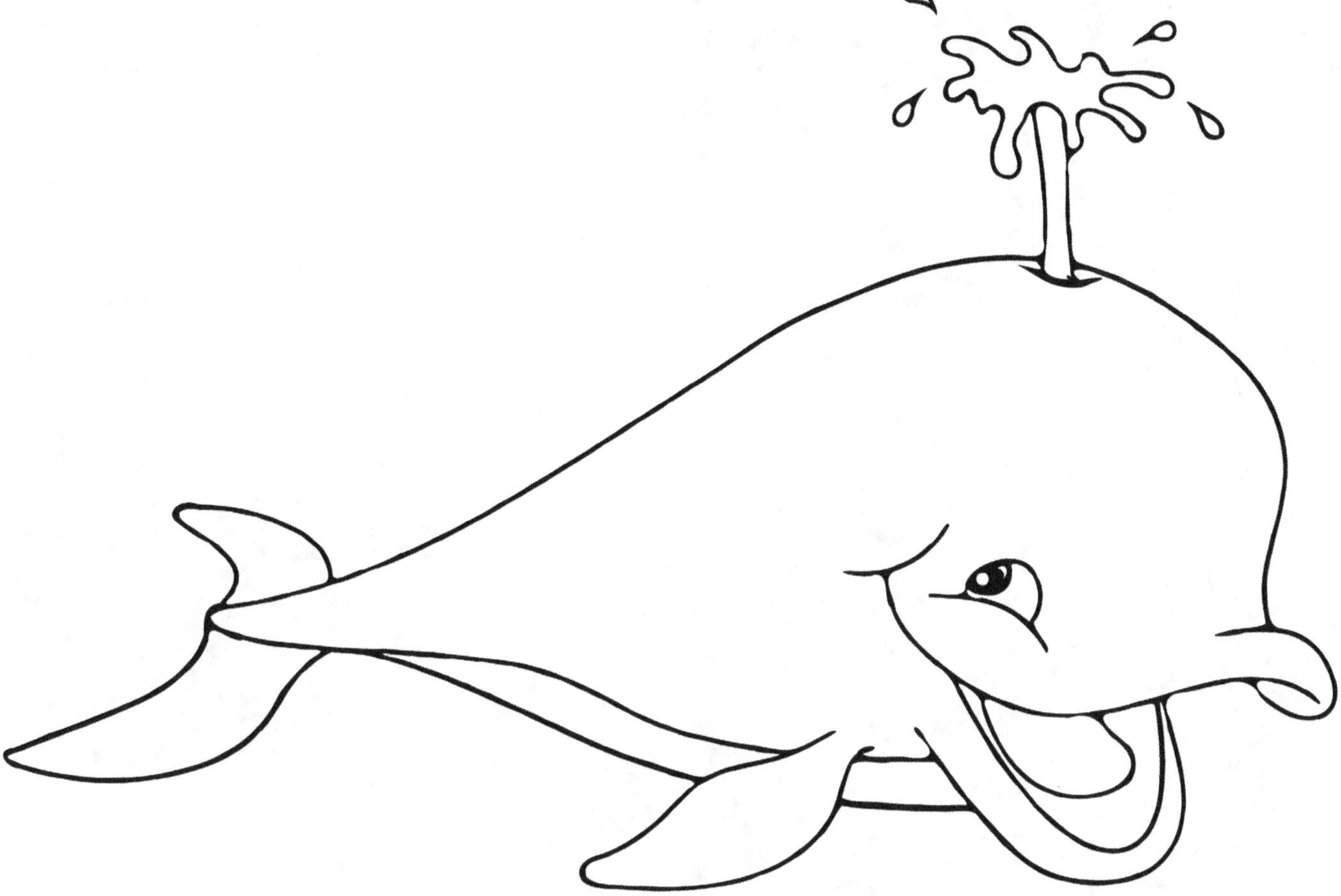

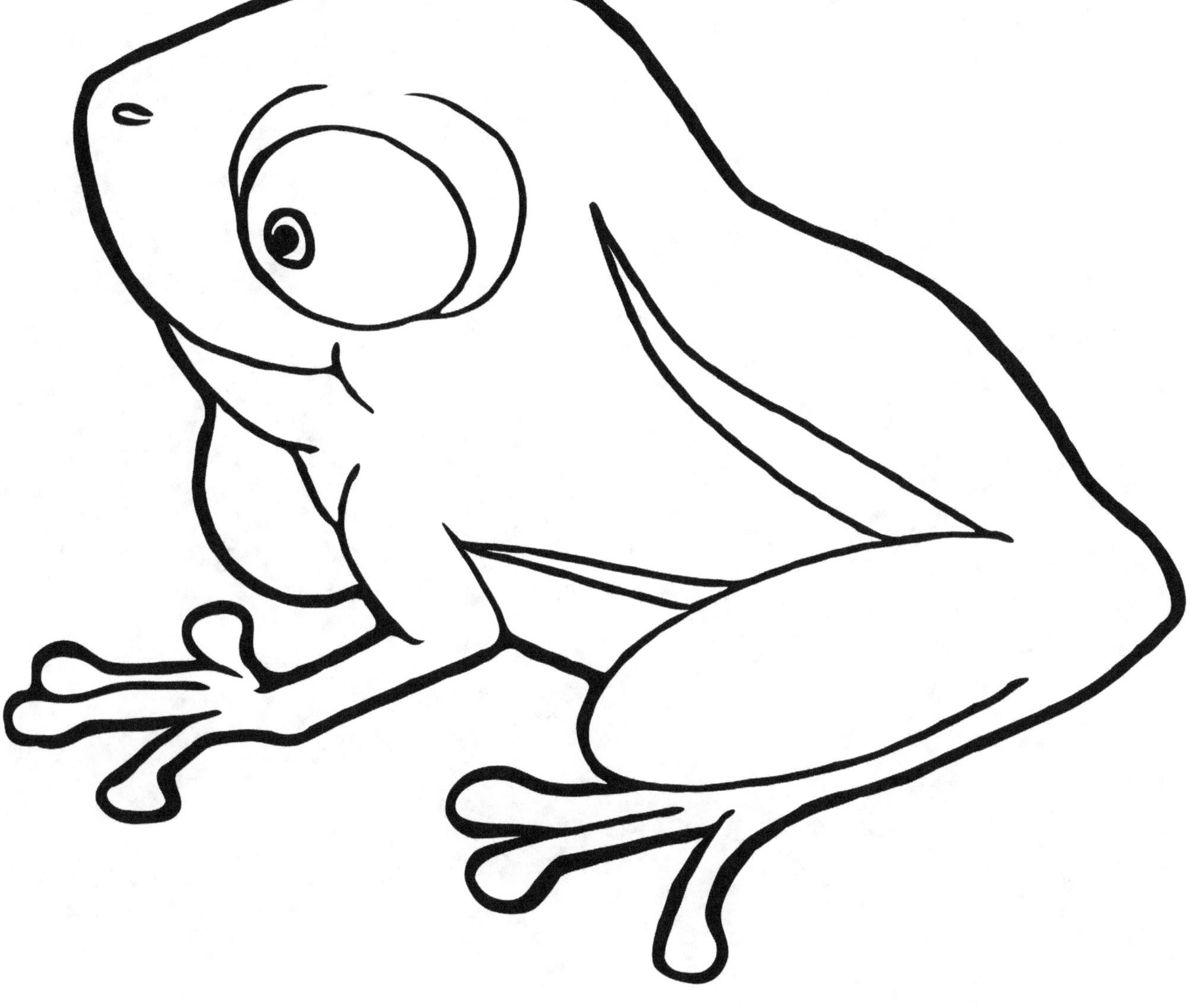

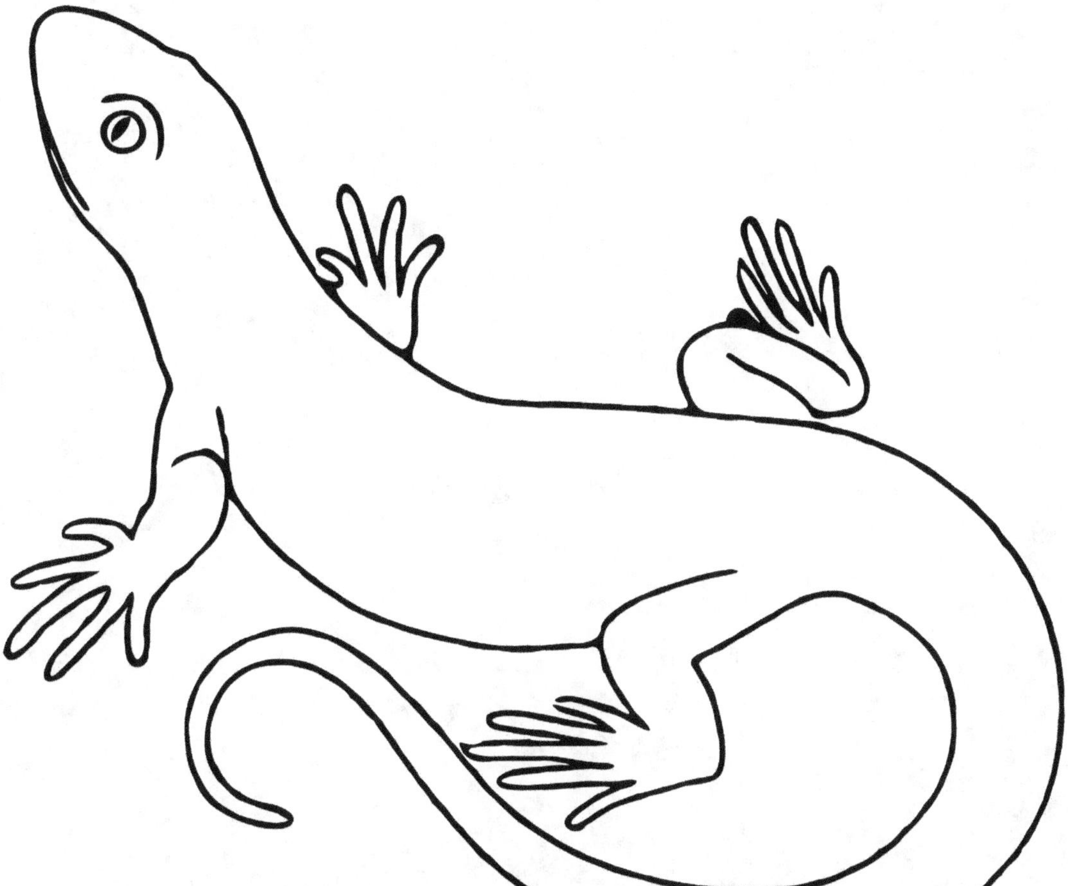

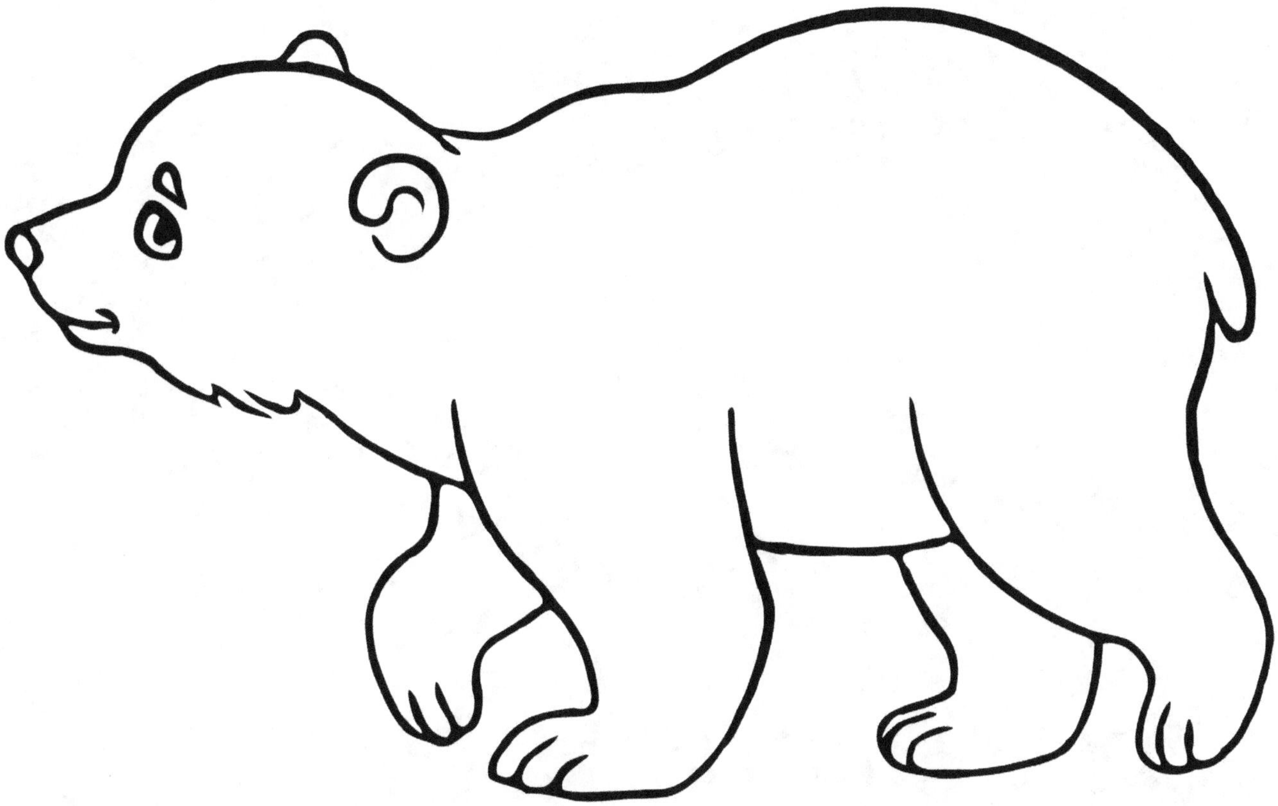

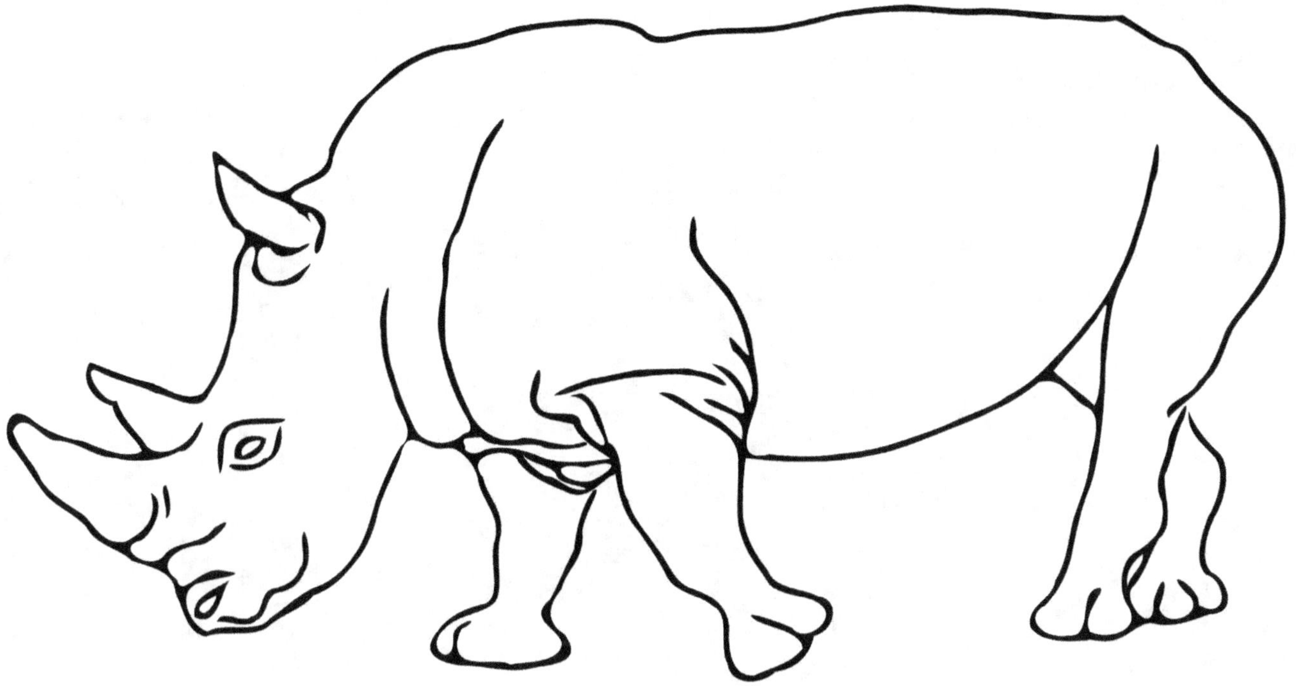

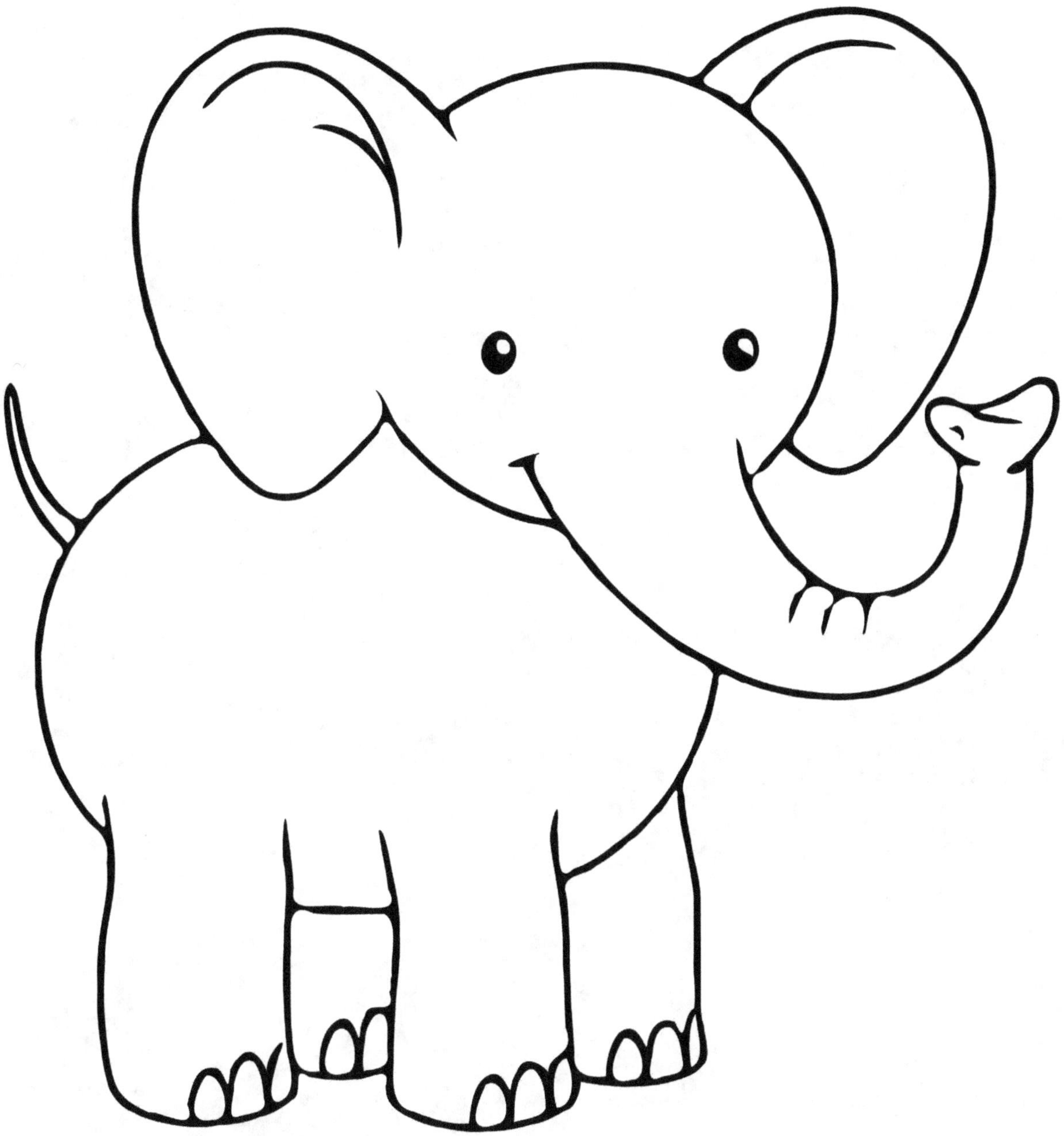

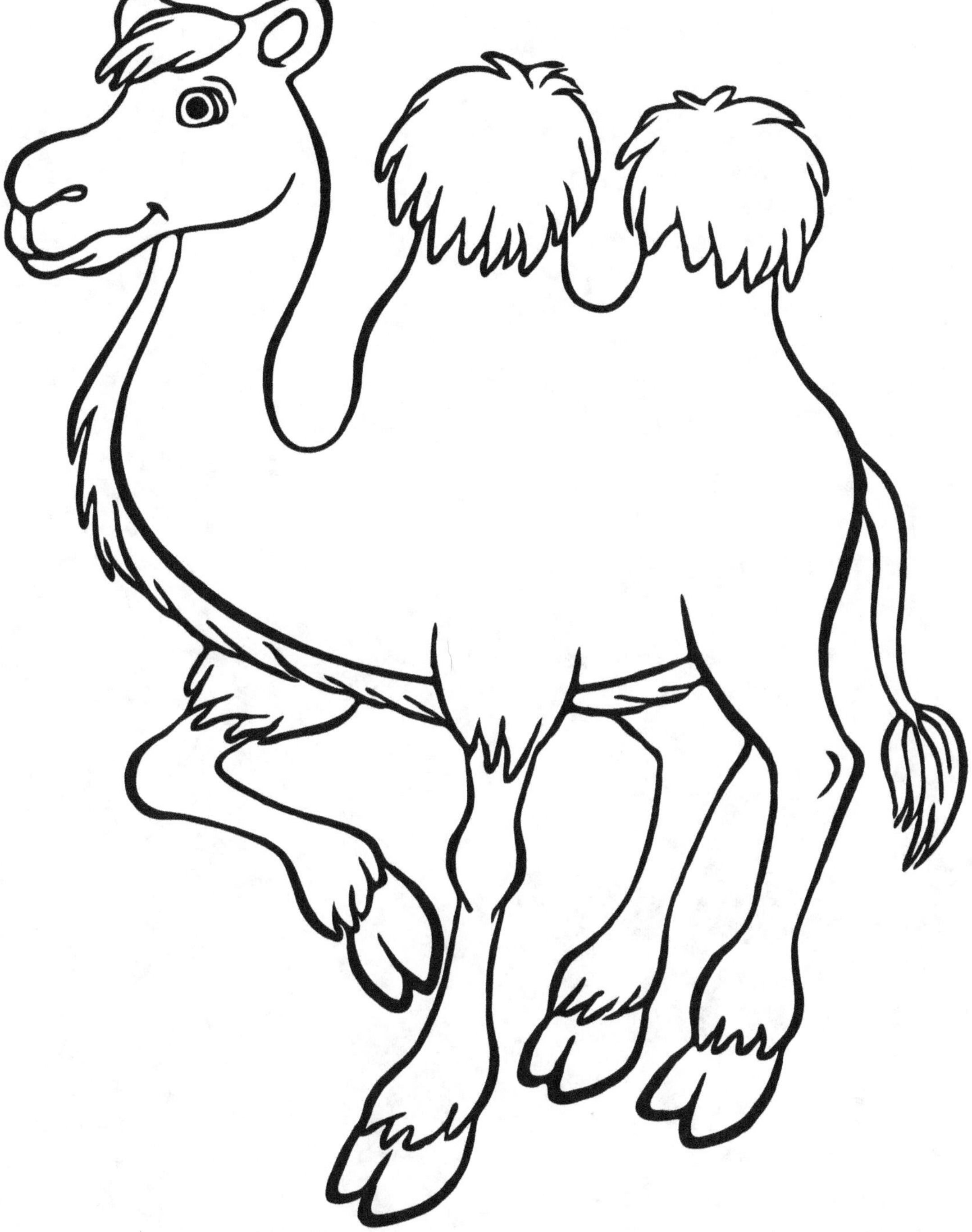

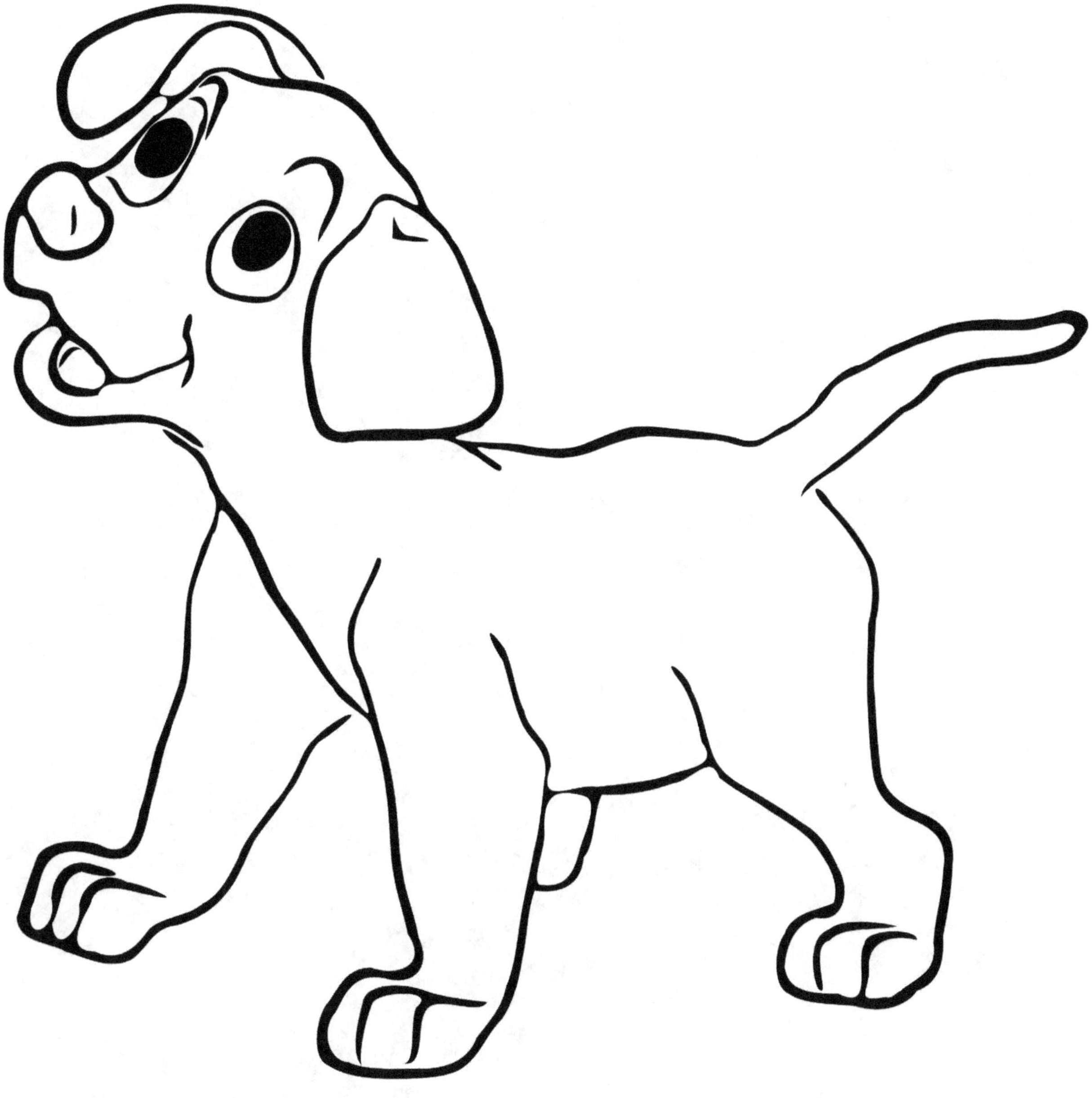

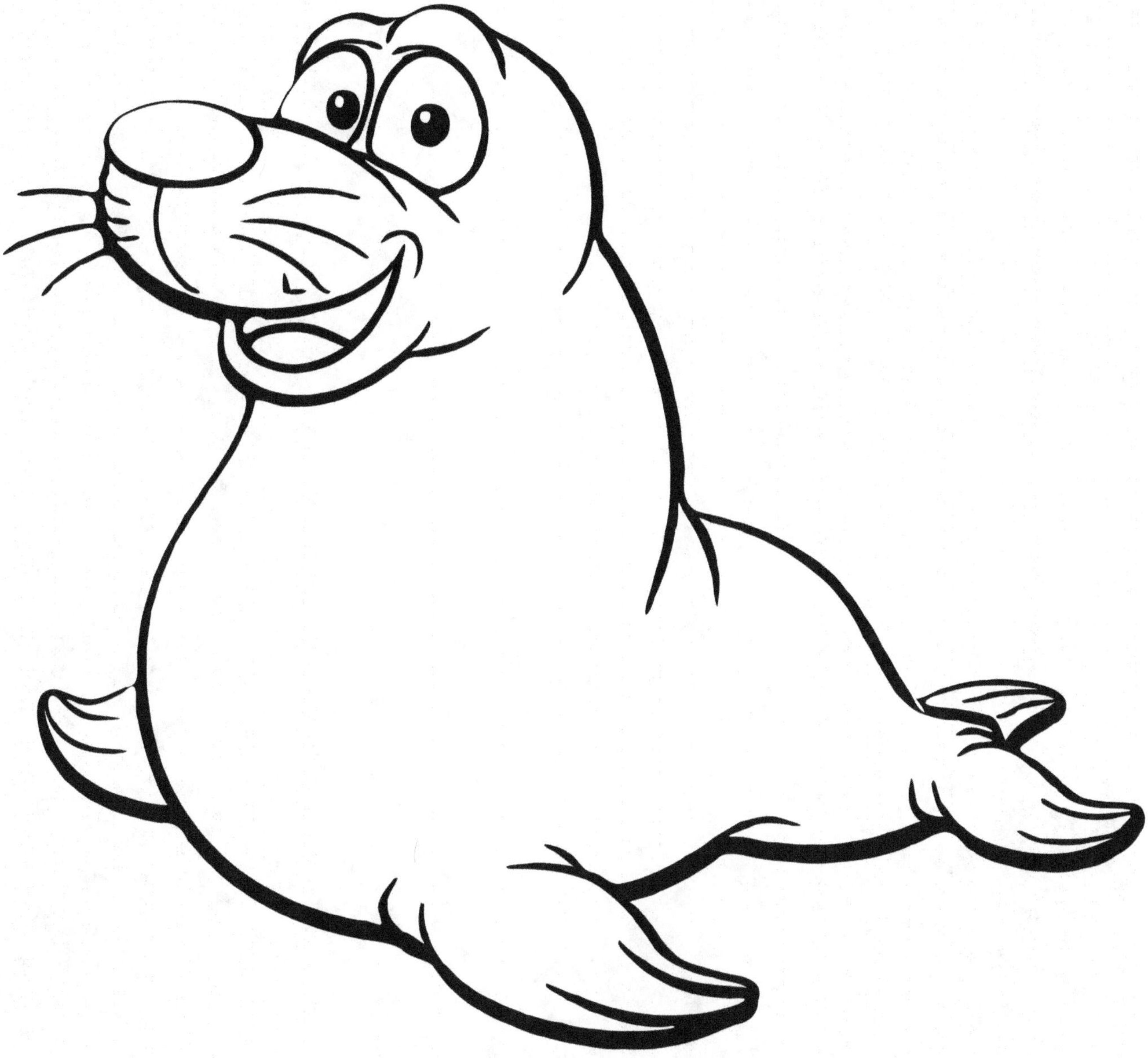

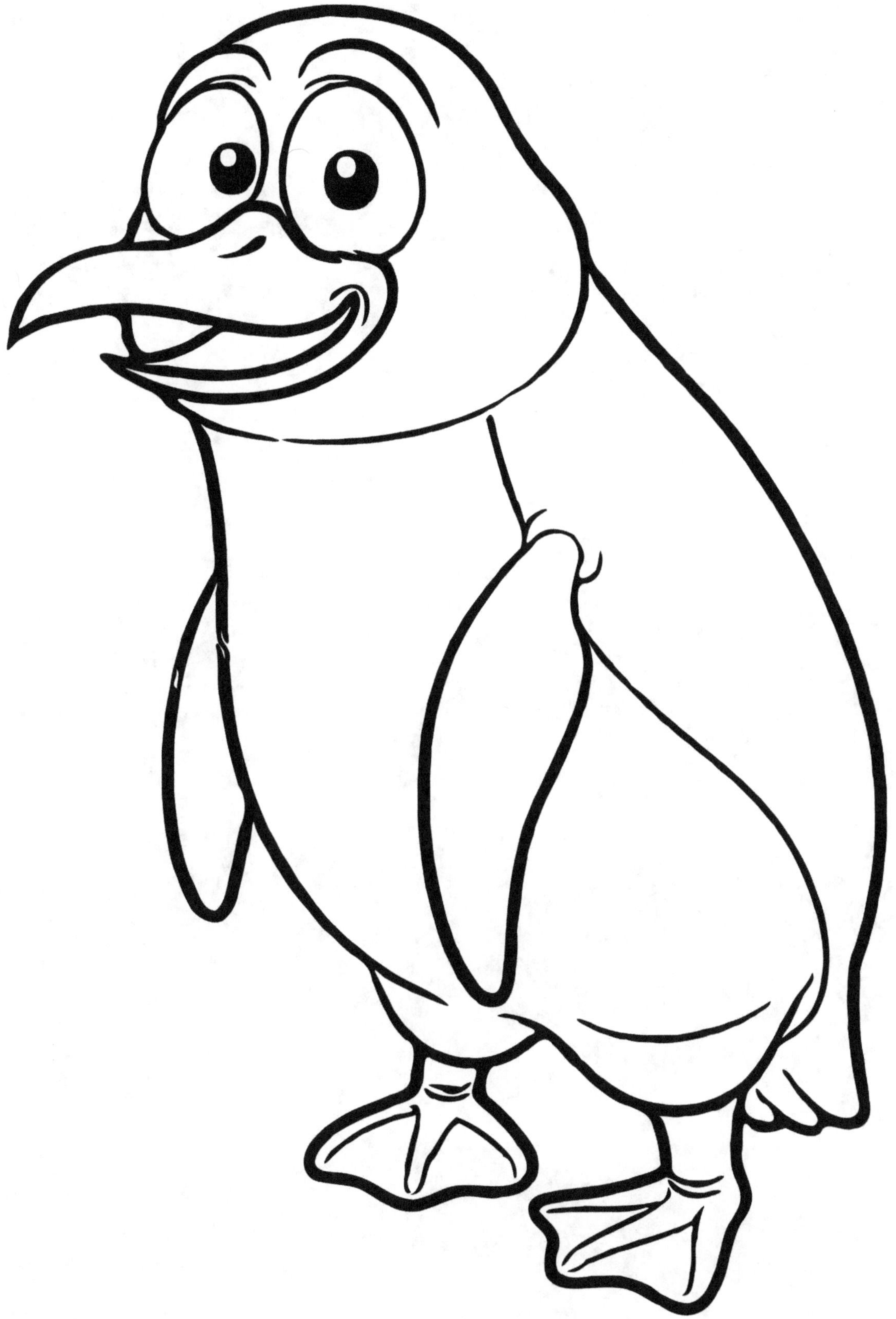

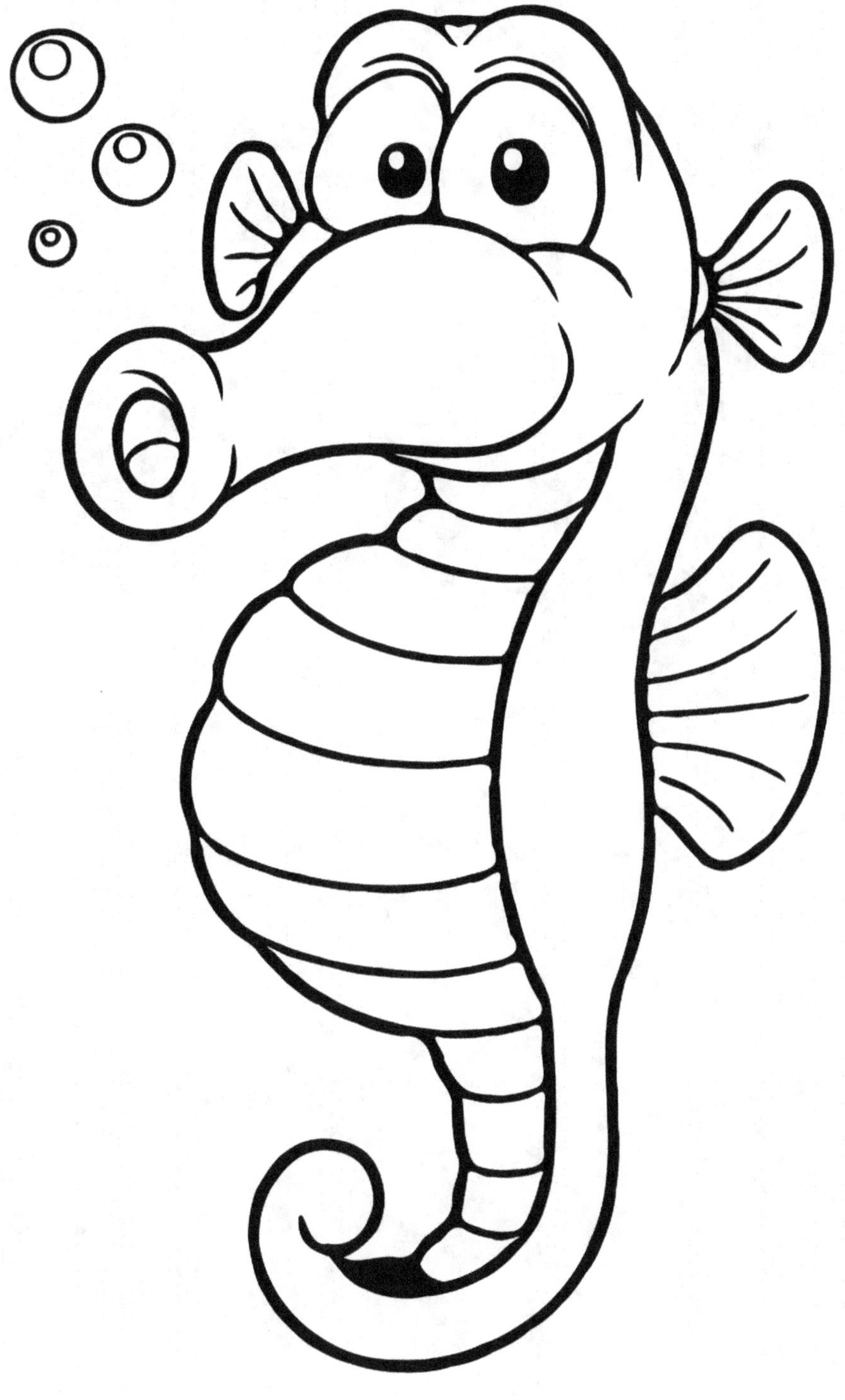

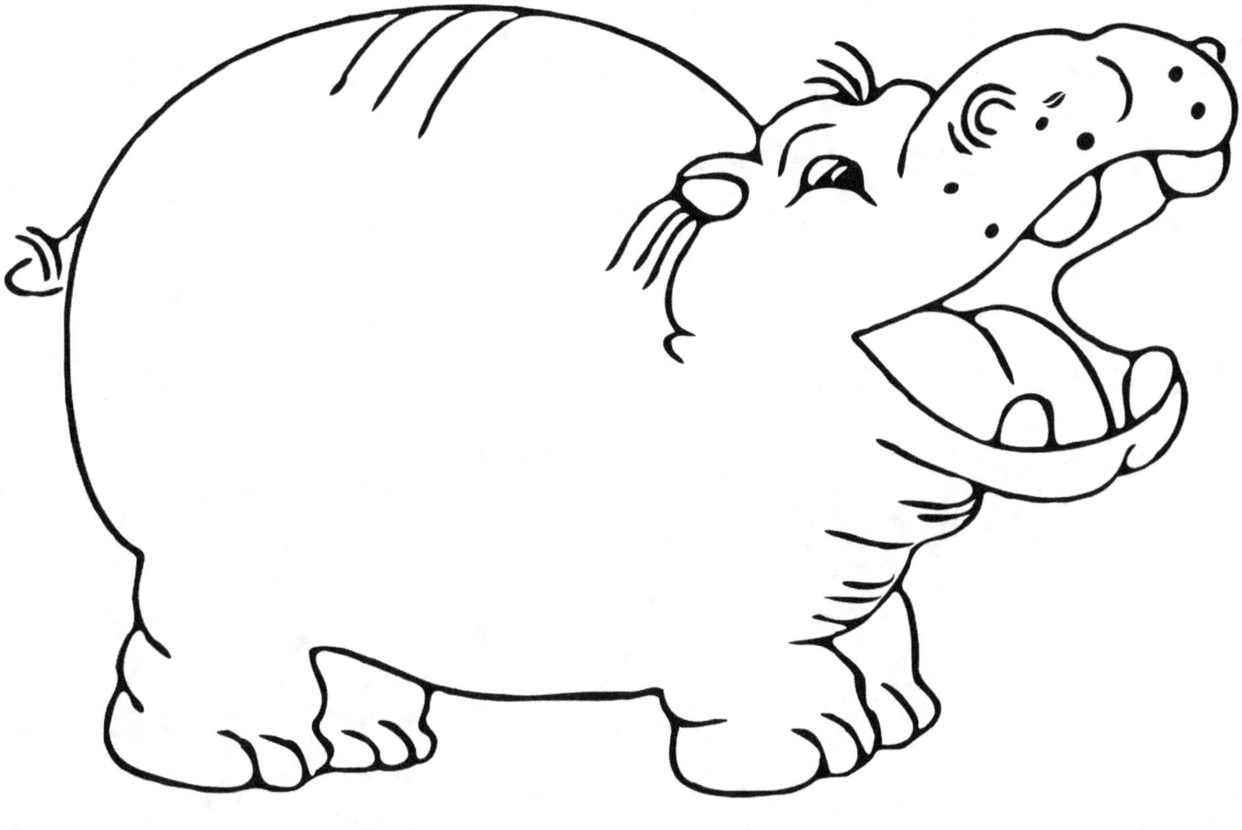

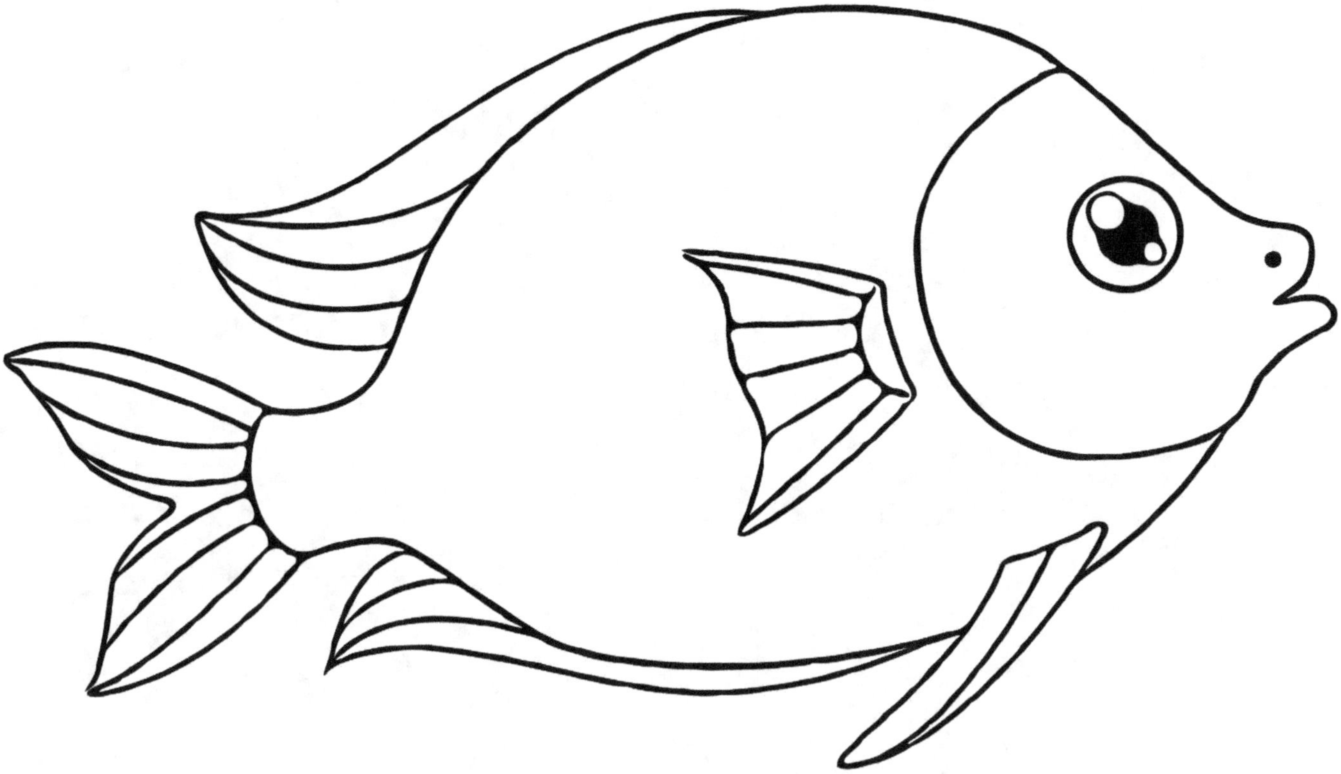

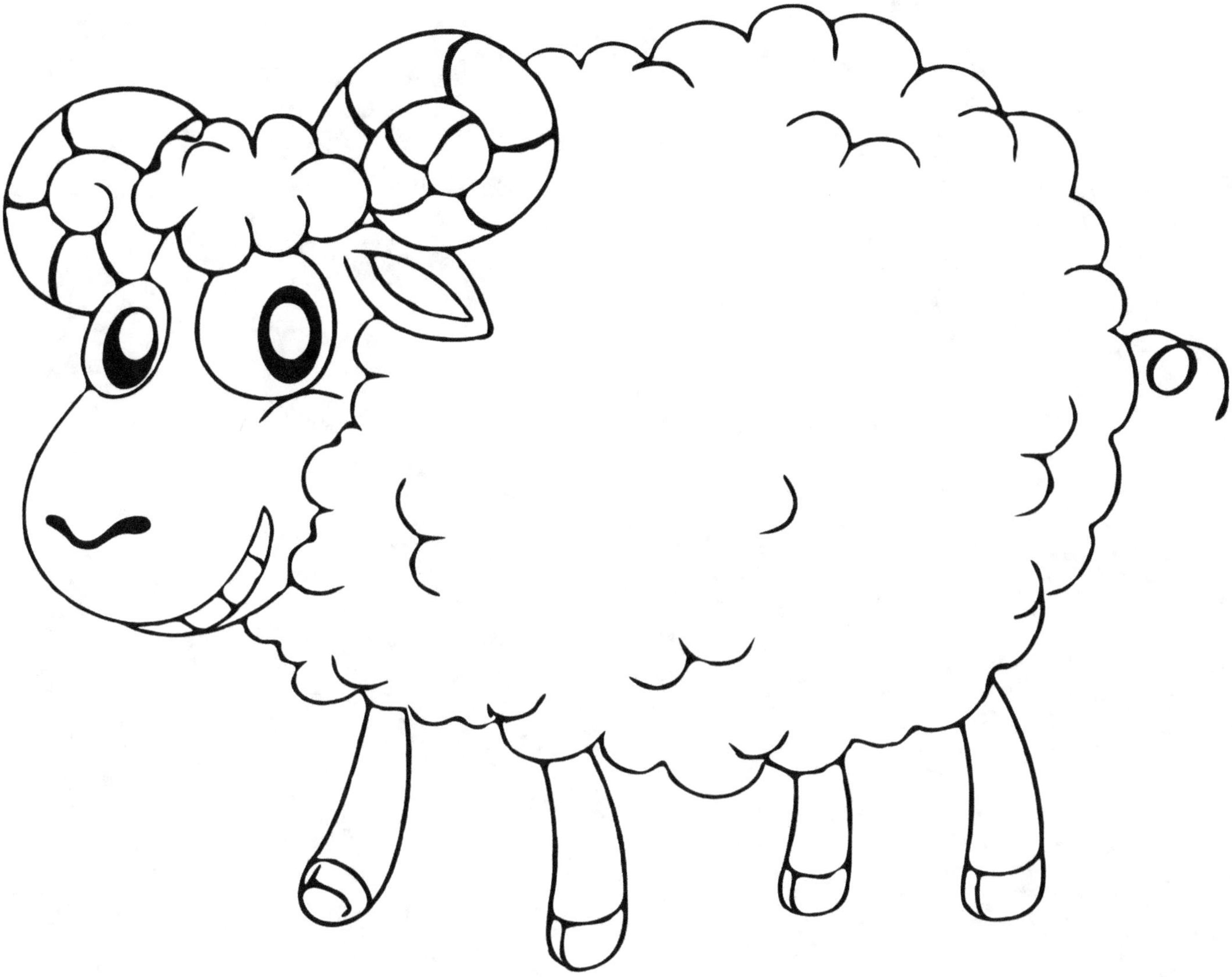

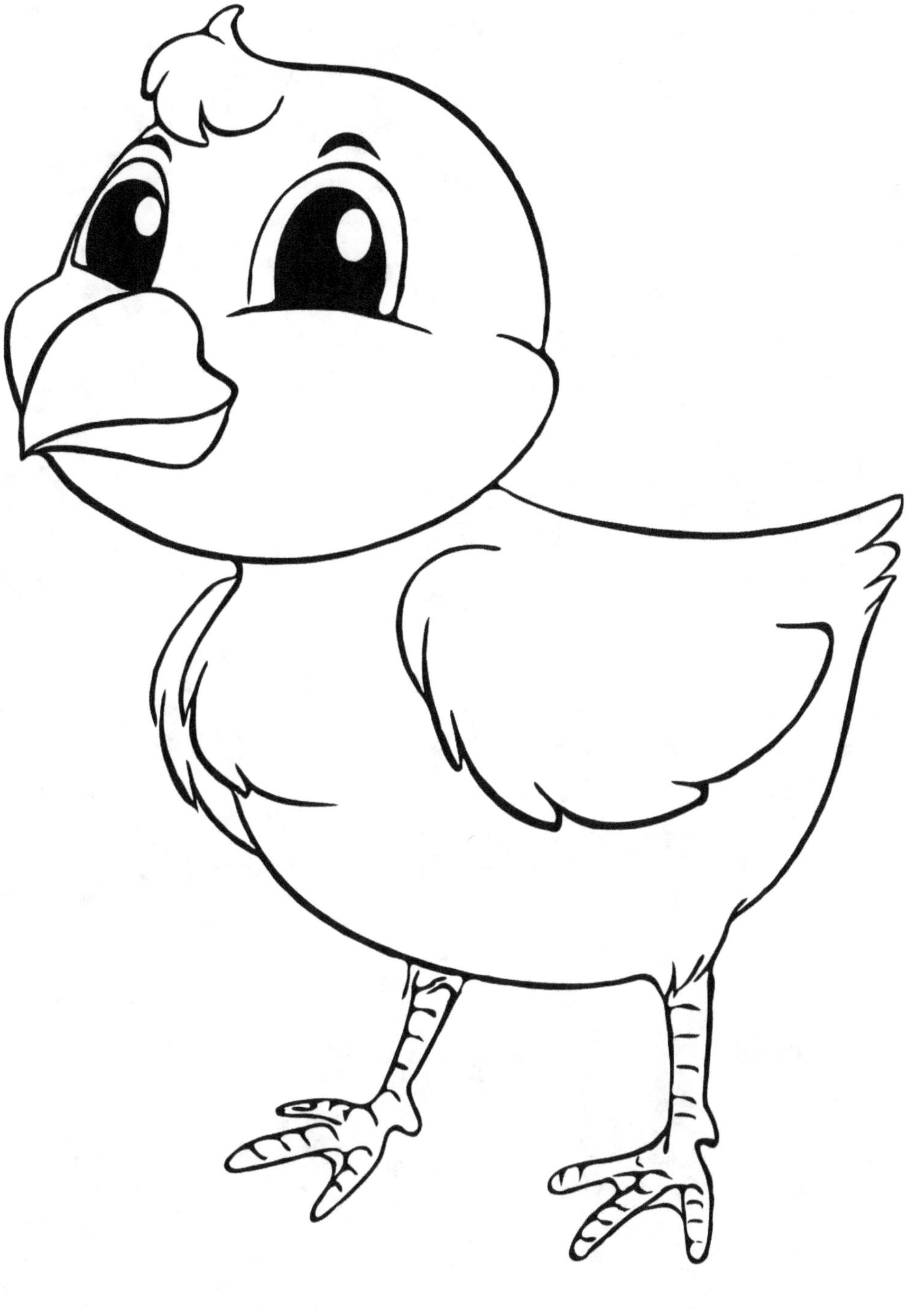

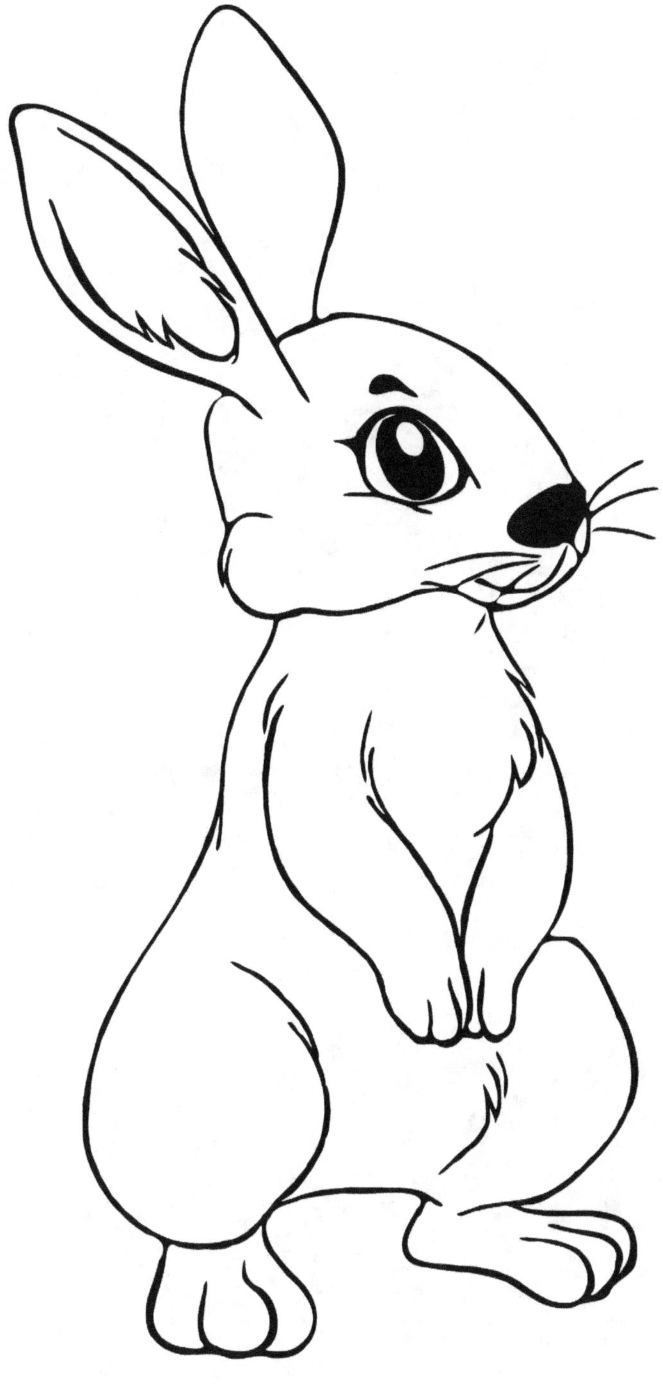

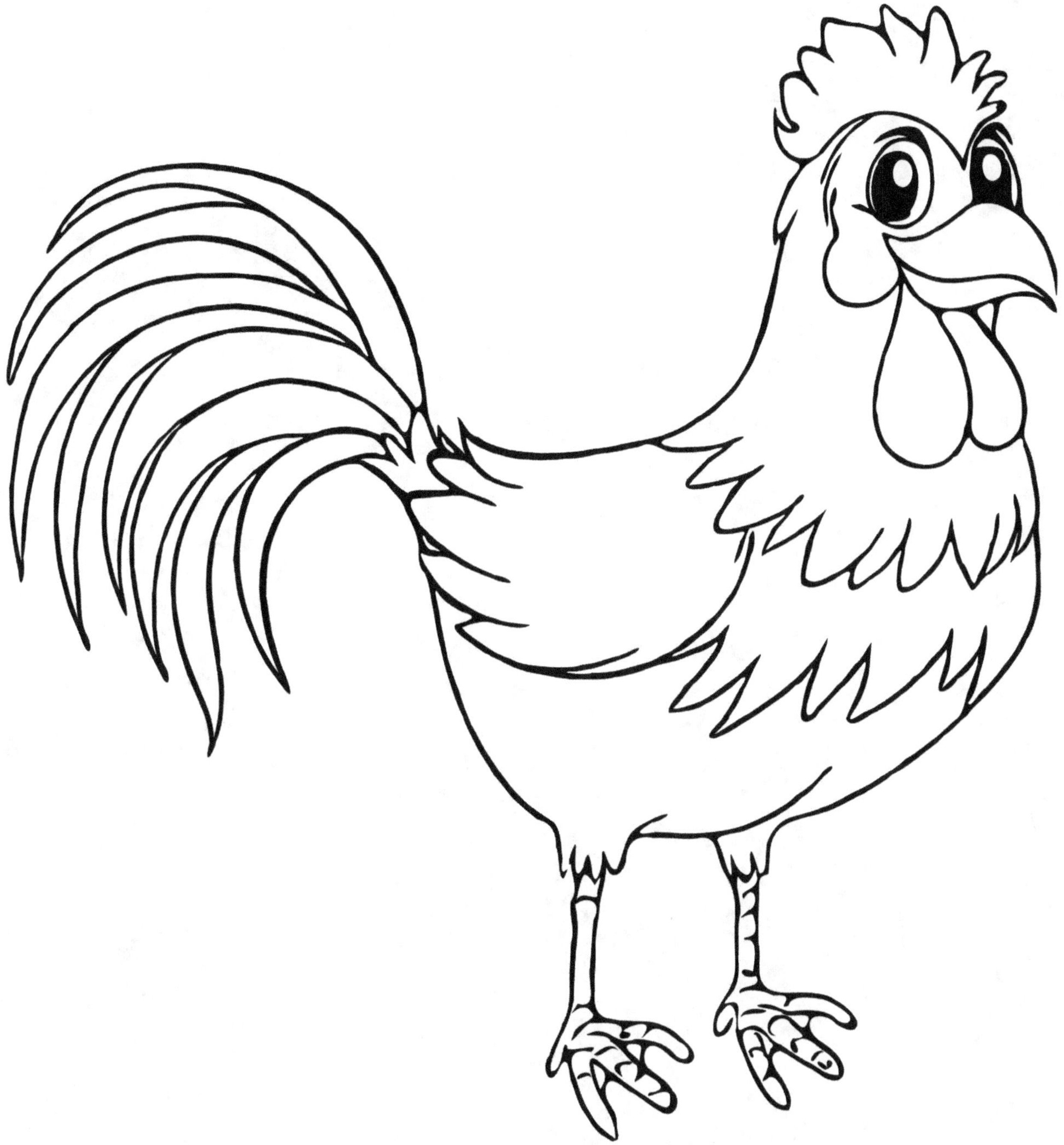

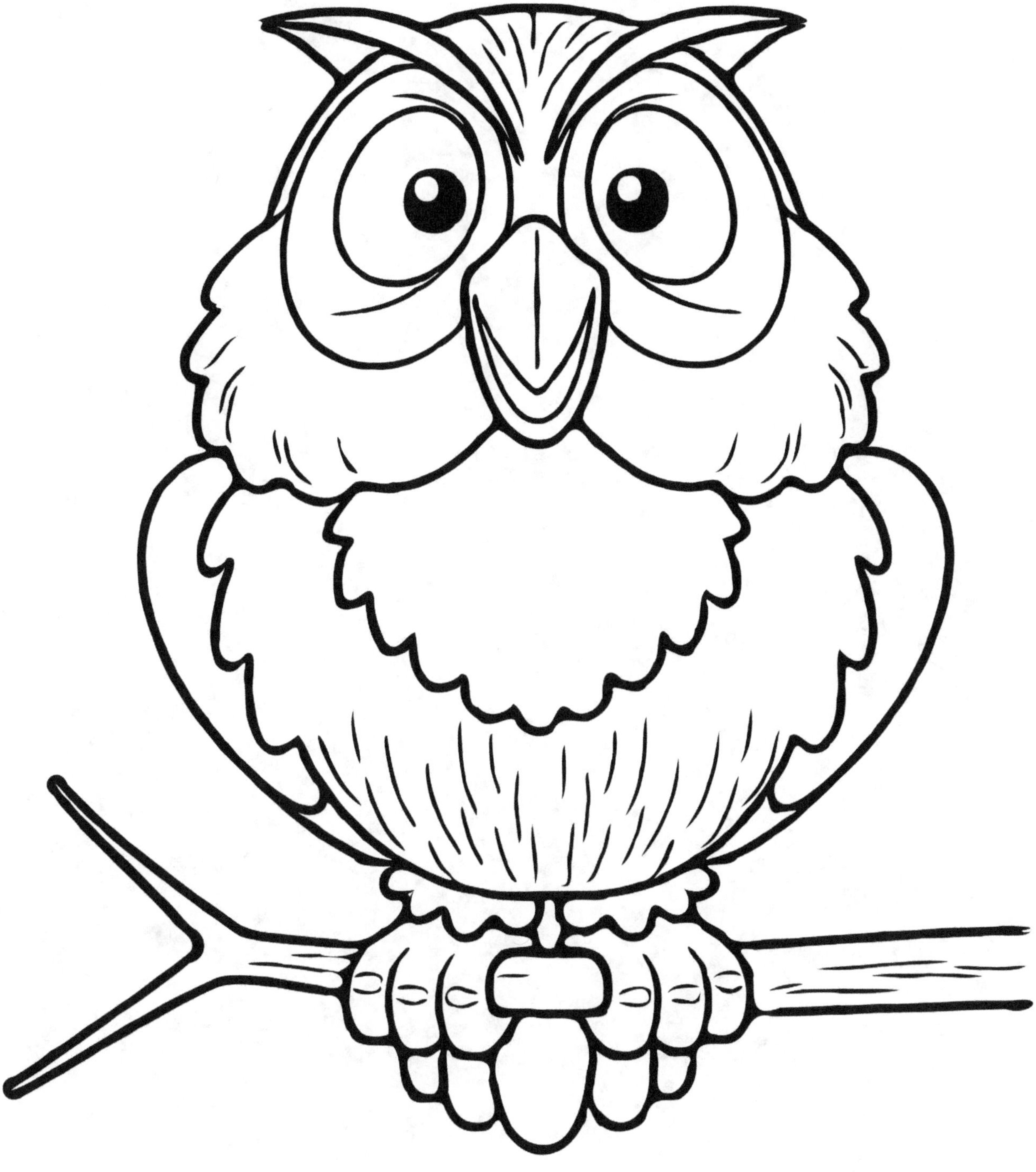

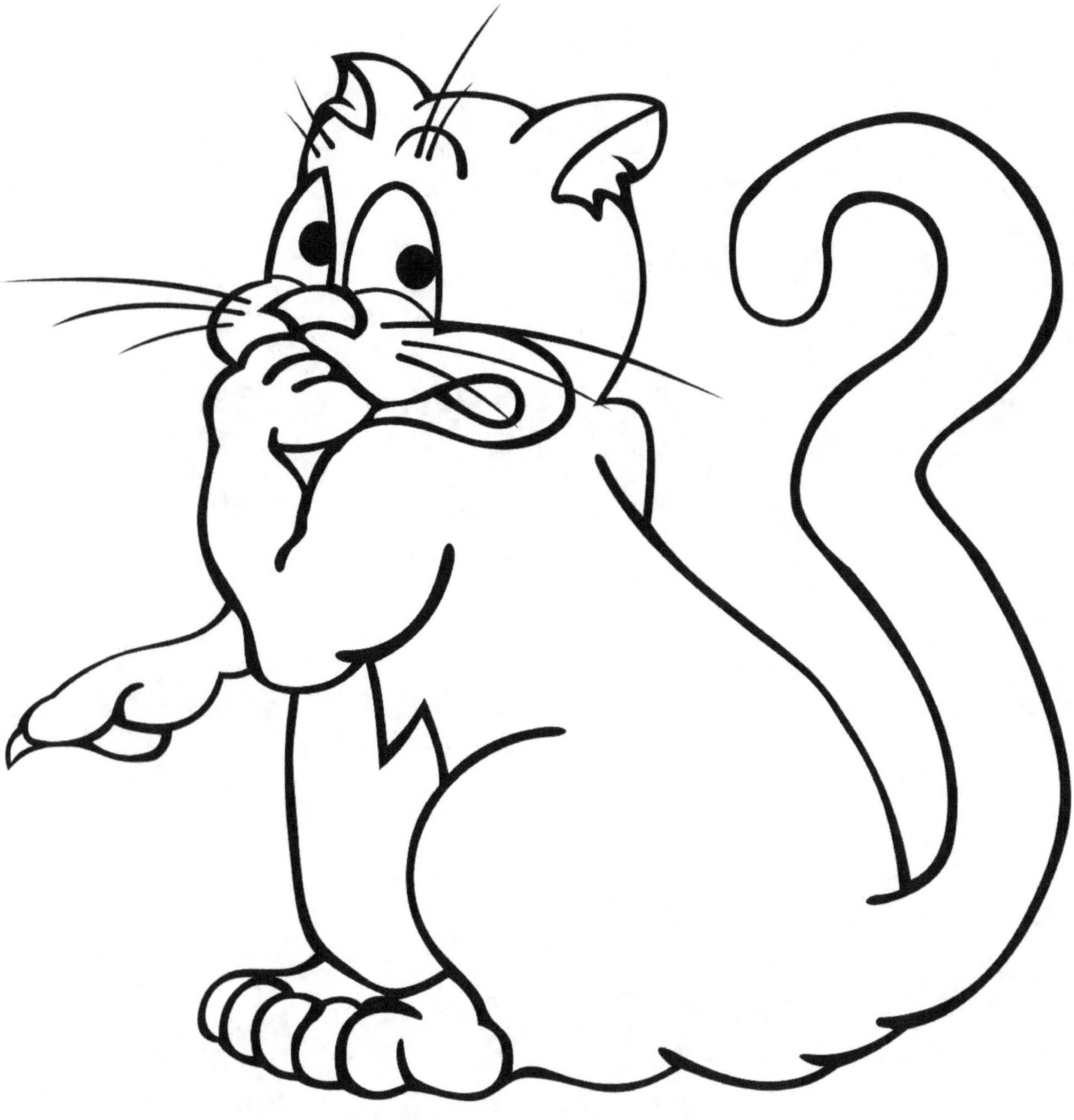

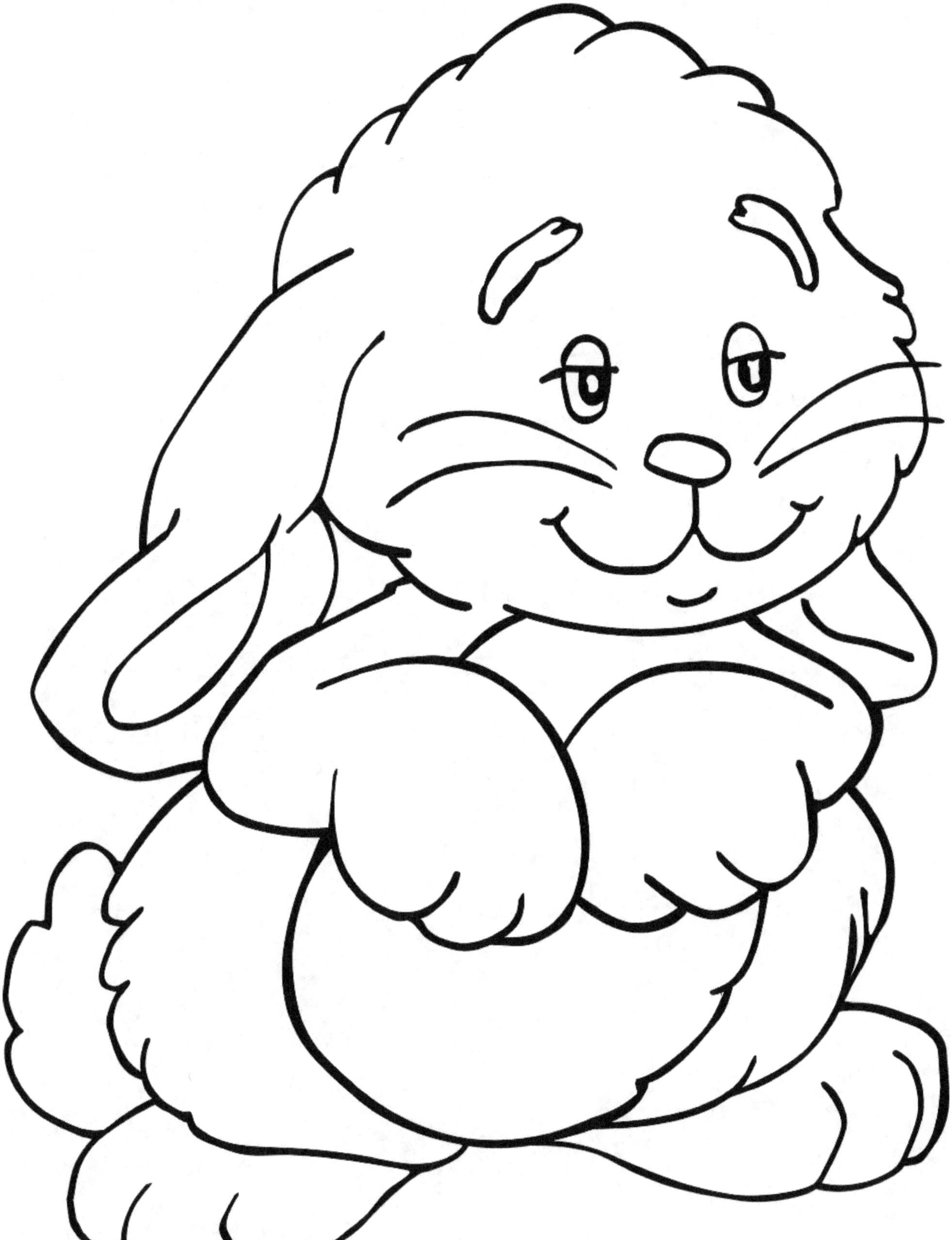

www.ingramcontent.com/pod-product-compliance
Lightning Source LLC
Chambersburg PA
CBHW081458220526
45466CB00008B/2695
* 9 7 8 1 6 5 5 2 3 0 9 6 7 *